Created for WORK

**Practical
Insights
for Young
Men**

Bob Schultz

GREAT
EXPECTATIONS
BOOK CO.
Eugene, Oregon 97402

Scripture quotations are taken from the King James Version of the Bible.

Created for Work
Copyright © 2006 Bob Schultz

Text Illustrations by Emily Schultz
Cover Design by Alpha Advertising
Interior Design by Pine Hill Graphics

Publishers Cataloging-in-Publication Data
(Provided by Cassidy Cataloguing Services, Inc.)

Schultz, Bob.

   Created for work : practical insights for young men / Bob Schultz. —
1st ed. — Eugene, Ore. : Great Expectations Book Co., 2006.

   p. ; cm.

   ISBN-13: 978-1-883934-11-8
   ISBN-10: 1-883934-11-7

   1. Work—Religious aspects—Christianity. 2. Work—Biblical
teaching. 3. Young men—Conduct of life. 4. Christian life—Biblical
teaching. I. Title.

BT738.5 .S38 2006
248.832—dc22   0601

Printed in the United States of America.

10 11 12 13 14 15 16 17 / 15 14 13 12 11 10 9 8 7 6

Dedicated to three boys who have brightened my life by their desire to work—Nathan, Paul, and Davey

Introduction

On the desk beside me lies a favorite old book published in 1861 entitled *Self-Help*. An Englishman named Samuel Smiles wrote it to encourage working men. Its four hundred pages are filled with one example after another of courageous men who overcame tremendous obstacles to benefit their socieites. Smiles wrote,

> Hugh Miller [a well-known man at the time]...stated the result of his experience to be, that work, even the hardest, is full of pleasure and materials for self-improvement. He held honest labor to be the best of teachers, and that the school of toil to be the noblest of schools—save only the Christian one—that it is a school in which the ability of being useful is imparted, the spirit of independence learned, and the habit of persevering effort acquired. He was even of opinion that the training of the mechanic, by the exercise which it gives to his observant faculties, from his daily dealing with things actual and practical, and the close experience of life which he acquires, better fits him for picking his way through the journey of life than the training afforded by any other condition.

In the education of boys today we've lost the importance of work as a most effective tutor. What is the good of knowing how to read or write if a young man doesn't have the heart to work, to produce, and to create? Boys are often forced to sit for hours, year after year, in front of books. Modern child-labor laws hinder and even prevent them learning to enjoy strenuous work. Then, after twelve to sixteen years of inactivity, folks wonder why all their teenager wants to do is sit on the couch playing games.

A boy who loves to work will master math when it's needed. He'll put out the effort to read what's important. In the meantime, his interaction with things that are "actual and practical" will provide the wisdom he needs to direct him into useful pursuits, and empower him to provide for a family of his own in days to come.

Within every man is the desire to work and produce. Some men don't even know that it's there. However, when necessity or some pressing authority pushes him into a useful position of employment his sense of work comes alive. I've employed many lazy boys who couldn't imagine work as something other than a necessary evil required to gain money for a toy. However, given time and proper instruction, these lazy lads have turned into dynamos working for the simple pleasure of work, disregarding the hardships and the pay.

This book is an attempt to express a biblical perspective of work and the richness of life it brings. It's written in a format for boys, yet it touches the fiber of older men and was first taught to my wife and three daughters.

I hope that *Created for Work* encourages you to appreciate your Creator Who is always at work and Who has made you in His image.

Contents

Art in Your Heart 11

Confidence 15

Dangers of the Diligent 19

Difficulty 25

Dirt 29

The Doorway to a Heart 33

Exit Strategy 37

Great-Grandpa Cornelius 41

Grudges 47

Increase 53

Initiative 57

Maintenance 61

Me Own Dog Tucker 67

Transported with Delight 73

How Could It Be My Fault? 79

My Instructor 85

Plodding 89

The Plumbline 93

Promptly After, But Not Before 99

Sidestepping Discouragement 103

Keeping Your Word 107

The Donut Race 113

The Making of a President 119

The Morning Song 125

The Process 131

Treasure in Our Box. 137
Understanding Your Boss 141
Unemployed? 145
Vision 151
What Are you Going to Do? 155
When Mercy Goes to Work. 161
You're Rude. 167
Work Within the Rules 171
Finish It. 177

Work while you work, play while you play.
That is the way to be cheerful all day.
All that you do, do with your might.
Things done by halves are never done right.
One thing each time and that done well
* is a very good rule as many can tell.*
Moments are useless trifled away; so
* work while you work and play while you play.*

—M.A. Stodart

Art in Your Heart

"Didn't you plan to be an artist at one time, Professor?"

Carver smiled. "I am an artist...I make beauty instead of recording it. There is beauty in well-tilled fields, in healthy and happy people, beauty to living in harmony with others. With God helping me, I have tried to create beauty according to His directing."

—From *Carver of Tuskegee*

God didn't have to put intricate designs on the wings of moths and butterflies. He could have made them all gray. He didn't have to paint a frog's eyes gold. He could have made them all black. God adds distinct and beautiful touches to each thing He makes.

His energy and creativity are without measure. They overflow into everything He does. Drudgery and bare minimums have no part in His work. Whatever He makes is not only useful, but also beautiful and fascinating. Some things He makes are very simple. Yet even their simplicity is a work of art.

God puts His heart into His work. He doesn't finish things just to get them over with. He commands us to do the same, "And whatsoever ye do, do it heartily" (Colossians 3:23).

My neighbor Medard lives part of the year in Poland and part in the United States. The last time he returned, he told me that the

Polish society is gray. According to Medard, they live without clear truth or error. They removed God from their minds and thereby lost the meaning and purpose for life. The workers are dull and poorly skilled. They do as little as possible and half-heartedly at best. Stripped of the awareness of God, Polish life, as Medard sees it, becomes a gray fog.

When my daughter Emily writes to a friend, she often spends as much time addressing the envelope as she takes to write the letter itself. Her overflowing heart cannot stop with just a destination and a return address. She must embellish capital letters with swirls and loops. Sometimes she fills them in with her colored pencils and designs a fitting picture that brings a smile to everyone who sees it.

I talked with the father of a girl to whom Emily writes. He said it didn't matter what was in the letters; the envelopes were enough to inspire him. If Emily doesn't add any artwork, and only writes the address on the envelope, her beautiful penmanship alone turns an ordinary letter into a keepsake.

Is Emily wasting her time and energy by putting her heart into her envelopes? Folks who live in a hurry might think so; folks who only consider production may consider it overkill. However, should they receive one with their name on it, the hurried sink into rest and the thought of production is forgotten in a moment of beauty. That's the way God is.

Minutes ago, a doe leading two fawns stopped four feet from my office window. The hair on her hide flowed in river-like curves around her legs and shoulders. I could have drawn a perfect line where the coarse brownish hair stopped on the outside of her leg and the soft tan hair began on the inside of her leg. What artwork! She's a prime example of our Creator, Who does all things well.

Unlike God, our energy and resources have limits. Still, He desires each of us to put what we do have into our work. "And whatsoever ye do, do it heartily, as to the Lord" (Colossians 3:23). Whatever you do, add that touch of abundance, that splash of overflow that comes from a heart filled with God.

When Al Gamache repairs my car, he fixes the initial problem first. However, he doesn't stop there. He's fixed a tear in the seat, tied up a loose hose, and secured the battery. Sometimes he's washed the car so it comes back looking sharp as well as running great. Al doesn't charge for the additional things, nor does he mention them. I have to discover them on my own. They're expressions of a man who likes to give more than is required of him, just like his God.

When Al gives me more than I need or deserve, it prompts me to pay him more than he charges and to look around for something special to give him, like a loaf of my daughter's freshly baked bread.

A society of people with full and abundant hearts gives the way Jesus commands, "Give, and it shall be given unto you; good measure, pressed down, and shaken together, and running over, shall men give into your bosom. For with the same measure that ye mete withal it shall be measured to you again" (Luke 6:38).

A society with empty hearts gives only what is required, and that grudgingly. They even cheat one another by giving less than is required. Then the cheated person cheats in return. Mistrust grows. Rather than giving out of the abundance of their hearts, they try to fill their empty souls with what they take from others, hoarding what they have gathered.

These folks become gray and lifeless. They lose the joy of life, because they have lost the God of life. Stingy folks stoop lower than an old blackberry bush. For in the right season, even a bramble gives berries to anyone who wants to pick them. That's God's overflowing nature.

How does this lesson fit into your life? Maybe your job today is mowing the lawn. Go out there and put as little effort into it as possible, as many boys do. Make boring laps, feel dull and wish you were somewhere else. Mow most of it. Don't care if you leave a few clumps standing tall. Shove the mower into the middle of the garage and return to slouch on the couch. Does that sound like an abundant life? It's not, yet many young men live a life like that. What a gray existence.

Learn to put abundance into what you do. When it's time to mow the lawn or accomplish any project for that matter, get after it, put your heart into it. Use your imagination. Instead of going around and around just like every other time you mow, why not try cutting it on an angle? Make two laps around the outside as usual and then cut the rest with diagonal stripes starting from one corner and going to another. Next week try a different design. Landscapers say it's good for the grass to be mowed in varied directions. It looks sharp too!

Practice mowing as if you were driving a car, keeping a straight line. See if you can mow without missing any of the grass on the turns.

If the garage is a little messy, you might develop a mowing station where you keep the mower, gas, and other yard supplies in an orderly fashion.

You don't have all the time in the world nor the resources like God does. You won't be able to accomplish every idea you imagine. Nevertheless, if you put your heart into your tasks, to the limit of what you do have, work changes. Instead of being a boring act of gray drudgery, it blossoms into creative color. It becomes an experience with your Maker. He's always on the lookout for men who will join Him in this abundant and overflowing life.

What do the men who team up with God receive? They obtain the joy of His presence and find favor with nearly everyone they meet.

The same imagination God used while creating the creatures that decorate the earth is available to you, to decorate every task you undertake.

And thou shalt make holy garments for Aaron thy brother for glory and for beauty. (Exodus 28:2)

Questions

- Why does God add beautiful touches to everything He makes?

- Why did Poland seem gray to Medard?

- Why does Al fix some things without charging?

- Think of the chores you have to do each day. How could you add color to one of them?

- Why does God want you to put your whole heart into whatever you do?

Confidence

All our fret and worry is caused
by calculating without God.

—Anonymous

Floyd Bowen is the best finish carpenter I've ever met. He has high standards and an eagle eye for plumb and level lines. He's always looking for new tricks, tools, and products to pick up his pace. Customers trust his judgment for woodworking trim styles and sizes. He accommodates other subcontractors. Floyd's methods are often faster, more accurate, and require fewer tools than those described in woodworking magazines. Besides all this, he's pleasant.

Two months ago, Floyd and I installed a handrail system and curved window casings in a new residence. During one of our early morning conversations, Floyd confided in me that he had lost his confidence. He seriously questioned his abilities and feared going to work.

Floyd! The best! How could he lose his confidence? When he began to think he had fewer skills than I did, I knew he was in trouble.

Did I think any less of Floyd? Not at all. Almost every man I know goes through times of losing his confidence. I do it myself.

One night I worked alone, trimming a house. My watch said nine o'clock. My energy dwindled. Only two pieces of baseboard needed installation and I could go home. They were tricky pieces; I just couldn't cut them to fit. One piece went between a curved fiberglass shower and what appeared to be a ninety-degree corner. My attempts to cut that piece failed repeatedly. A fear came over me that I would never get out of that bathroom! I took another trip to my saw, then another and another.

"I can't do it!" I said. However, I had to finish that night and no one else was there.

I learned some things about confidence while playing high school baseball. I got plenty of hits but they always went to right field. My coach blamed it on my slow swing. But when we played against McKenzie High School, the reason for my trouble became clear.

Tim, McKenzie's pitcher, was the fastest in our league. He could throw a fastball past most of our best hitters, strike after strike.

The first time at the plate, I hit the ball so hard it knocked down the shortstop. My next hit went out into left field for a single. My third swing sent the ball all the way to the left center fence! How could this slow right-field hitter blast Tim's fastball almost out of the park? My shocked coach asked, "What's happened to you?"

The answer was simple. "Confidence." Tim was the only pitcher in the league that could control the baseball. I had complete assurance he wouldn't hit me. With other pitchers, I feared being hit. The wilder the pitcher, the more I thought about the ball hitting me, rather than me hitting the ball. However, with Tim it was different. When he started winding up, I started swinging. I trusted his control, kept my eye on the ball and hit away.

At the root of Christianity is the belief that the God Who created the universe controls it. Every life event thrown to you and me comes from the most controlled Pitcher in the world.

When a Christian begins to lose confidence, it's often because he's lost sight of God's control. False, fearful ideas creep into his mind where thoughts of safety and courage belong. He starts to think that events happen by chance instead of under the watchful eye of God.

The first step back to confidence is telling God the details of your life—what's happening and what you think about it. Instead of struggling, running, crying, or hiding, stop; quietly open your heart to God. There is a tendency in all of us to run when we get scared. Running only increases our trouble. The night I worked in the bathroom installing baseboard, I felt that urge to run. I wanted to hurry and get out of there. That made me unable to concentrate on my work. I needed to slow down, tell God my trouble, and then quietly measure and cut.

Isaiah 30:15,16 described me, "For thus saith the Lord GOD, the Holy One of Israel; In returning and rest shall ye be saved; in quietness and in confidence shall be your strength: and ye would not. But ye said, No; for we will flee upon horses; therefore shall ye flee: and, We will ride upon the swift; therefore shall they that pursue you be swift."

Returning to the simple belief that God is in control, telling Him every detail of my trouble and resting in His care is the greatest source of my confidence.

Sometimes I lack confidence to start complicated woodworking projects. However, if I boldly attempt the obvious steps, when the difficult steps arrive God usually has given me the wisdom to accomplish those also. By the time I get my tools unloaded and my saws set up, I have an idea of what to do next.

Joshua didn't know how the Israelites were going to cross the Jordan. When they put their feet in the water, the river upstream stopped. A dry path opened before them and they walked across. It worked for Joshua and it works for me.

Sometimes a man loses his confidence when he has been away from his work for a season. An injury, a vacation, a layoff can all get a man out of practice and unsure of his abilities. Floyd knows if he takes a vacation from finish carpentry work, it takes two or three days to tune up his skills again once he is back on the job. He expects it, begins slowly, and with effort gets back up to speed.

This happens to students the first week of school after a summer vacation. Maybe you too doubt yourself, "Will I be able to do the math I did last year?" Sure you will. However, it might take some review to polish up your skills.

When your assurance shrinks from lack of practice, it's easy to remedy. Start doing it again. When temporarily laid off from a job, keep practicing the skills you need for it. If you can't actually do the work, read about it and mentally go through the processes. Clean your tools. Be ready to start again when the opportunity arises.

God desires His people to live with poise. When you find yourself backing away from your responsibilities because of fears, stop struggling. Tell Him the details of your trouble. Rest. Take the next step you know to take. Regain your skills when you can.

After a couple weeks of questioning, Floyd's confidence returned. He stepped up to the plate and hit the fastballs of woodworking. He continues to be the best finish carpenter I know.

How about you? Where is your confidence? "Batter up!"

> **For the LORD shall be thy confidence, and shall keep thy foot from being taken.** (Proverbs 3:26)

Questions

- What is confidence?

- What did Floyd feel like when he lost his confidence?

- Why could I hit Tim's fastball?

- Have you ever lost your confidence?

- How do you get it back when you lose it?

Dangers of the Diligent

*The moral flabbiness born
of...success.*

—William James

Jack Loy was a night owl. Long after others went to bed, his mind continued to plan, to prepare, and often to pray. Therefore, when he needed a part-time job he naturally hired on as a night watchman for a rent-a-cop company. Jack drove around town at appointed times, checking buildings. He looked for suspicious characters and kept alert for signs of fires, unlocked doors, and anything that might endanger the property of the clients who hired his services.

One morning, between two and three o'clock, Jack nosed his car into the Volkswagen dealership on Coburg Road. While searching for criminals among rows of beetle bugs and vans, he noticed lights inside the showroom. Detective Loy investigated the scene.

Jack found the owner sitting behind his desk. Afraid that someone might be stealing one of his cars, the rich man couldn't sleep. He got out of bed and came down to the car lot to protect his goods. This man had more money than most of us will ever see, and he feared losing it.

Solomon wrote, "...the abundance of the rich will not suffer him to sleep" (Ecclestiastes 5:12). This car dealer, by steady careful effort, built a profitable business and became very wealthy; however, he faced one of the trials of the rich: *How do I keep what I have?*

Folks that care about their things tend to be more prosperous than those who don't. As their goods increase, there are more things to care for. In time, the fruit of the diligent can become the cares of this world, choking the Word from their hearts.

Deuteronomy 6 warns us that when our houses are full of good things and we have eaten and are full, "Then beware lest thou forget the Lord." It's our nature to be sidetracked by the things in this life, whether they come as gifts or from our hard work. The diligent must be on guard.

Industrious workers face many temptations that slothful workers don't. Proverbs 22:29 says, "Seest thou a man diligent in his business? he shall stand before kings; he shall not stand before mean men." A man careful in everyday affairs rises to places of leadership. His character places him with rulers and he often becomes one himself. As the head and not the tail, he encounters a new set of temptations ordinary laborers don't.

Proverbs goes on to explain these temptations, "When thou sittest to eat with a ruler, consider diligently what is before thee: and put a knife to thy throat, if thou be a man given to appetite. Be not desirous of his dainties: for they are deceitful meat."

I remember from my childhood a jar of home-canned green beans sitting on our pantry shelf. My sisters remember it too. Those beans were the only food in the house. We didn't have to use self-control to keep from eating too much meat or hold ourselves back from a second piece of cake. There was no meat. There wasn't any cake either. We ate vegetables, not because we should; we ate them because we could. Nobody had to warn us about the dangers of overeating. You're never tempted by something that isn't there.

Things have changed. Today, I can go to the store and buy almost anything I want to eat. I didn't face that temptation as a child. If I don't control my appetites, I'll fail to finish life well.

Most men do not reach their full potential until later in life. God takes years to build talents, attitudes, and visions in men. He also takes years to outfit them with resources. There's a time when all that you have learned, all that you have earned, and all that you are comes side by side with the needs of others. Like a farmer patiently waiting for his harvest, God waits for His work of planting, watering, fertilizing, and weeding to yield useful fruit within

us. As an older man's steady, careful effort aligns with God's work, the crop in his heart matures.

The Bible tells us of two such men. Nehemiah, faithful as a cup-bearer to the king, was ready when it came time to rebuild the walls of Jerusalem. Caleb, faithful through forty years of wandering with whiners in the wilderness, was ready when it was time to conquer the mountains of Hebron.

Sadly, David, though faithful through years of difficulties, gave in to his appetites when he had the resources to do so. As king, he had the power to get anything he wanted. Instead of using that power to benefit his people, he used it to fulfill a lust.

When you reach the time of life when it all comes together for you, when resources, talents, and opportunity meet, will you be self-controlled? Will you hold a knife to your ever-present appetites? Will you hear God's voice and respond with instant obedience? Will you use all that you have and all that you are to produce good fruit? Or will you take your resources, meant to feed the Lord's household, and eat and drink them yourself?

This is an important lesson, because few men finish well. The temptations of life change as you develop. If not alert, you'll slowly slip into the next season of life where the paths that were once safe to walk are now lined with traps.

That grand quality of diligence, which is essential when you begin working, turns a man into a workaholic if not balanced. The freedoms that bless the industrious become snares when given to selfish pleasure. The diligent are tempted to forget God, trust in riches, and look down on the poor. What once was the reward of hard work quickly transforms into the resources to fulfill the lust of the flesh, the lust of the eyes, and the pride of life. Be on guard.

God designs the diligent to collect resources and talents with the goal to use them in an appropriate season for good. As always, Jesus leads us by His example. After thirty years of obscurity, the season for Jesus' public ministry drew near. In the wilderness, He faced and over-came the temptations of appetite and power. After overcoming, He used His resources to "preach the gospel to the poor...heal the bro-kenhearted...preach deliverance to the captives...recovering of sight to the blind...set at liberty them that are bruised... [and] preach the acceptable year of the Lord" (Luke 4:18,19). Jesus, having all the resources of the universe, didn't use them for selfish pleasure. At the appointed day He saved the world, rather than give in to this world's pleasures.

Like Jesus, Nehemiah, and Caleb, your season to produce fruit will come. When it does, may you be the man who refuses the cares, riches, and pleasures of life. May you be one who in an honest and good heart, hears the Word, diligently keeps it and by God's grace brings forth a bountiful harvest one hundred fold.

> *And beside this, giving all diligence, add to your faith virtue; and to virtue knowledge; And to knowledge temperance; and to temperance patience; and to patience godliness; And to godliness brotherly kindness; and to brotherly kindness charity. For if these things be in you, and abound, they make you that ye shall neither be barren nor unfruitful in the knowledge of our Lord Jesus Christ. But he that lacketh these things is blind, and cannot see afar off, and hath forgotten that he was purged from his old sins. Wherefore the rather, brethren, give diligence to make your calling and election sure: for if ye do these things, ye shall never fall: For so an entrance shall be ministered unto you abundantly into the everlasting kingdom of our Lord and Saviour Jesus Christ.*
>
> (2 Peter 1:5-11)

Questions

• Why couldn't the owner of the car lot sleep that night?

• Where will the diligent stand?

- What dangers do the diligent face that the slothful don't?

- What happens if you do not put a knife to the throat of your appetites?

- Every man should be a diligent worker. In what other areas of life should he display diligence?

Difficulty

First a thing is impossible, then
it's difficult, then it's done.

Chaos. Frustration. Pressure. These words describe the atmosphere at my current job. This week I'm installing cabinets in a large, expensive house. The whole project is costing more than imagined and taking longer than it should. If you visit this job site during a workday, within minutes of arriving, you'll overhear some worker grumbling to another about the materials, the management, or their lack of money. Complaining slithers into every conversation.

Into the middle of this muddle entered Lawrence. His company makes countertops for kitchens and bathrooms from slabs of solid granite. In this particular house, the kitchen island looks like a fat music note. It's straight with a round eating area attached to the end.

Cutting a three-foot circle out of a one-inch thick piece of rock isn't easy because stone saws are designed to cut straight lines.

"That's going to be a challenge for you," I lamented as he measured for the top. He replied, "That's what makes us good!"

Through the years Lawrence has faced many hard-to-cut shapes. Daring to accept those challenges has developed his talent and confidence. Now he welcomes the demanding projects because he knows they will help him grow. For Lawrence, overcoming difficulties "makes us good."

Peter Wolf is one of the most respected handrail installers in town. A Wolf rail system is beautiful. Peter not only installs rail parts, he developed a shop where he makes his own rails and fittings. I've watched him take an old black-walnut tree blown over in a storm, mill it into boards, stack it to dry, and then years later turn it into a gorgeous curved handrail.

Peter didn't learn his trade by taking easy jobs. Twenty years ago his handrails were just straight sticks of wood mounted to the wall with a couple of brackets. When a builder wanted him to make a rail with a little more style, he did it. Through the years rails became more complicated. Owners and builders added starting steps, open rails with balusters, turnouts, volutes, end caps, and eventually fancy curves. Each time the job became more difficult, Peter needed new tools, new methods, and new tricks. Peter is an exceptional craftsman today because he accepted the challenges of increasingly difficult jobs.

To God, life is a growth process. In His design, growth follows difficulty. Therefore, without a challenge there is little or no growth.

Since growth requires difficulty, the boy who consistently backs away from it will fail to mature. If he avoids lifting tools and materials, he will continue living with weak muscles. If he avoids hard math problems, memorizing, and creative thinking, he will continue to own a weak mind. If he avoids life's challenges, he will have a weak spirit. By sliding down the easy paths of life, a boy remains or becomes feeble, frail, and effeminate.

In addition to growth, God tests the hearts and souls of men with difficulties. Our response to these challenges shows what manner of men we are.

Dave and Tom both plan to wash their cars on Friday afternoon. However, when Friday comes it's raining. Dave says, "I'm not washing that car today. I'll get wet and cold." Tom says, "What great weather to wash the car! Rain keeps the soap from drying. I won't have to rinse so often. Where's my sponge?"

Rain tested the hearts of Dave and Tom. Dave thought only of his own comfort. Tom had eyes to see past the difficulty to the benefits beyond.

Noah Webster said, "To overcome difficulty is an evidence of a great mind."

If that's true, welcoming trials and troubles as opportunities and friends is the pathway for developing a great mind.

The nation of Israel found themselves slaves in Egypt. Pharaoh gave them mud and straw and required tons of bricks in return—a difficult task. Then God hardened Pharaoh's heart so that Pharaoh required the same amount of bricks, only Israel now had to get their own straw. That seemed bad, but it was good. God wanted to get Israel in shape and He used Pharaoh as the coach! Later, when God led Israel out of Egypt, "He brought them forth also with silver and gold: and there was not one feeble person among their tribes" (Psalm 105:37).

A man of faith sees beyond daily events to the good God who controls all. Frequently God disguises Himself as trouble, problems, and difficulty. The wise look past those costumes and see provision, growth, and a good education.

All problems are reruns. Whatever hardship you face has been faced by someone before you. The faithless focus on the trouble and complain. The faithful thank God and overcome.

Mrs. Norman Rinehart is an old-timer in the Walterville area. She has a reputation for growing hearty tomato plants. When young Jennifer wanted to sell vegetable seedlings, she sought out Mrs. Rinehart's advice.

"What's your secret for growing healthy tomatoes?" Jennifer asked.

"I whack them every day," Mrs. Rinehart replied.

When the older woman watered the seedlings, she slapped her hand across their tops. She didn't uproot them by any means, but whacked them enough to inform them that they needed some roots to withstand the life ahead.

How do you respond when the difficulties of life whack you? I hope your faith is big enough to see that your current difficulties are not an accident. They come from God's hand. He's strengthening your roots for the future. Don't complain or back down.

I hope that when a challenge or a difficulty comes your way, you'll announce with men like Lawrence, "That's what makes us good!" and then overcome it.

> *He that hath an ear, let him hear what the Spirit saith unto the churches; To him that overcometh will I give to eat of the tree of life, which is in the midst of the paradise of God.* (Revelation 2:7)

Questions

- What is Mrs. Rinehart's secret for growing strong tomatoes?

- What did Lawrence say when faced with a difficult counter-top?

- What made Peter so good at building handrails?

- What happens to the boy who tends to pick the easy jobs?

- According to Noah Webster, overcoming is a sign of a _____.

Dirt

She objects to farming because she says it is dirty,
offensive work. There are parts of it that are dirty.
Thank God, it only soils the body, and that can be
washed.

—From *Laddie* by Gene Stratton Porter

Through years of installing foundations and framing houses, I've had many good employees. One of the best, Doug Jordan, earned a place in my Worker's Hall of Fame for his ability to get dirty.

Doug never went home with clean clothes. It didn't matter where we worked or what we did. He found some dirt and managed to get it all over himself. It really wasn't that he looked for dirt. He focused so intently upon his task that he gave little regard to anything else. Heat or cold, wet or dry, and clean or dirty didn't seem to register in his mind. If there was a job to do he stayed on it until he finished.

I remember seeing Doug crawl out from under a house, covered with dirt from head to toe. When he smiled, even his teeth were dirty!

One winter day we wallowed in the mud while pouring a house foundation. As the last driver washed his rig before leaving, Doug pushed a wheelbarrow up to the concrete truck. The driver filled the barrow with warm water. Doug, covered with muddy globs, climbed in, clothes and all. When he crawled out, his clothes were a uniform shade of brown.

Dirt never got in the way of Doug completing a job. I respected him for it.

When I was a fifth-grader, my family and I lived at the High Y Trailer Park in McKenzie Bridge, Oregon. My friends and I spent much of our free time making forts in the woods. We'd dig a hole about three feet deep, lay a piece of plywood or sticks over it, and then cover that with dirt and plants. At a glance, you couldn't tell it existed. We left an opening just big enough to slide into. That pit became everything from a dungeon cave to the hold of an old sailing ship.

If we weren't digging in the woods, we dug by the river. We made canals, little waterfalls, and small lakes from rocks and mud. I can't imagine life without digging!

Almost every boy I've ever met likes to dig. Set a toddling youngster loose in a garden. He'll stagger around a little, fall to his bottom and begin digging. He won't stop with just rubbing dirt on his legs and in his hair. Given the chance, he'll even eat it.

At a recent outdoor wedding reception, most of the well-dressed guests sat on white chairs near white-clothed tables by the lake. A short distance away, I spied a pack of boys. They had gotten off the lawn and found a dusty slope of rocks and dirt. Some fought their way up the hill while others tumbled to the bottom. I don't know just what they were doing; all I could see were boys in motion, a cloud of Central Oregon dust, and big smiles.

To gain my respect, a boy doesn't have to look like a pig returning from the wallowing pit. I take my hat off to any boy who can dress formally without squirming and complaining. However, he also ought to be content while covered with slime if a task requires it, like the respectable fellow who pumped our septic tank last spring.

A man needs the internal grit to stick his face into the dusty winds of adversity that blow through life. He also needs the determination to stick his hands into grease and mud to accomplish the assignments given him.

The man who stays close to the dirt tends to stay close to reality. There's something in farming, logging, or ditch digging that keeps his thoughts down to earth. The builders of the Tower of Babel got too far from the dirt and found themselves in trouble. "And they said, Go to, let us build us a city and a tower, whose top may reach unto heaven; and let us make us a name, lest we be scattered abroad upon the face of the whole earth...Therefore is the name of it called Babel; because the LORD did there confound the language of all the earth: and from thence did the LORD scatter them abroad upon the face of all the earth" (Genesis 11:4,9). There are benefits in staying close to the dirt.

God could have made man out of anything, but for some reason He picked dust. "God formed man of the dust of the ground, and breathed into his nostrils the breath of life; and man became a living soul" (Genesis 2:7). The only difference between a man and dust is the breath of God. The man who sees himself on the same level as dirt, were it not for the breath of God, has a healthy opinion of himself.

It's not that you have to live in good old farm soil to grow healthy. The point is, don't be too proud to get dirty and never let dirt stop you from accomplishing your tasks. Refusing a job because you'll soil your hands is the mark of a man who hides from life instead of one who dives in and conquers it.

If you are one of the millions of boys and men who enjoy dirt, remember that it doesn't belong everywhere. It's extremely thoughtless to walk onto a freshly mopped kitchen floor with muddy hunting boots or to jump into your friend's new pickup after walking on the beach without first brushing yourself off. A good man considers the property of others. Therefore, he'll try to keep his dirt to himself.

There are two things you never want to get dirty regardless of the job. One is your heart and the other is your mind. We tend to get things mixed up. There is a tendency for men to stay away from the dirt of hard work and then pollute their minds with pictures and imaginations. They won't get their hands dirty but find no objection to reading books or watching videos that foul their hearts.

God's man desires to keep his soul clean. Should he fail, he'll cry as David did, "Create in me a clean heart, O God; and renew a right spirit within me" (Psalm 51:10). Always choose to keep a clean heart even if it means having dirty hands and face. It's better to have an honest hardworking job than a dishonest easy one.

So the next time there's a grimy task, don't back away from it because you'll soil your shirt. If you have the chance, change into your work clothes. If not, risk a dirty shirt rather than fail to complete your responsibilities.

It's been years since I've seen Doug, yet I'll never forget his smiling, dirty face. He'll always hold an honored place in my Worker's Hall of Fame.

In the sweat of thy face shalt thou eat bread, till thou return unto the ground; for out of it wast thou taken: for dust thou art, and unto dust shalt thou return. (Genesis 3:19)

Questions

- What is the difference between dust and a man?

- What made Doug such a good worker?

- What parts of you should always remain clean?

- Why should a man never purposely get his home dirty?

The Doorway to a Heart

I want to see my business not just as a source of income, but as a way for me to express my love for life and for others.

—Cecil O. Kemp Jr.

Don Barton called this morning to ask if I would look at his house. Allergies are forcing him to move to the coast. He wants my help to make his home more attractive and sellable.

I met him at 9:30. We walked through each room, making notes of doors to trim, thresholds to install, and sheetrock holes to patch. After considering the needed repairs, Don took me up on his flat roof that seems more like a patio than a housetop.

The selling point for Don's house is the incredible view. Leaning on the rail three stories above the ground we gazed across the McKenzie Valley toward the small town of Walterville. Yellow maples and green fir trees separated the pastures and cultivated farms into patchworks. One hundred feet below, ripples in the river sparkled in the fall sun. The beauty before us and the sun soaking into our backs put us into a quiet reflective mood. We stared into the river like a couple of old hunters staring into a campfire. From time to time, we commented about our great God Who would make such inspiring scenes and about the creatures that walked or flew into view.

We began talking about events that took place years ago. We used to meet for breakfast at the Lucky Logger Restaurant on Saturdays. Over pancakes and eggs we shared life's adventures and the lessons God attempted to teach us through them. However, we came to a place where we chose different roads. It wasn't that we had an argument; we both maintained a mutual respect for each other, but our paths didn't cross much anymore.

We waved at each other while passing on the highway and spoke pleasantly when we met at the local fair or grocery store. We each had destinations and schedules that kept us moving and prevented us from having a conversation deeper than current events and the weather.

Today was different. Don needed my skill. I needed the work. God knew we both needed something more. As we enjoyed the beautiful morning and the inspiring view, I confessed to Don my shortcomings toward him. He sensed some of his own failures. We experienced the joy and oneness that follows confessing faults and offering forgiveness. When we parted, I climbed into my truck feeling full, clean, and happy.

God often uses work to put two people side by side. I don't think God cares as much about my carpentry skills as He does about the people I encounter each day.

Last spring, my friend Peter and I spent three months working together. Jobs had begun piling up for him. He called. I helped. When we finished them, I moved on. God has used Peter to mold my heart. Work is the excuse that brings us together. Peter knows how to install handrails, and I know how to help him. When God thinks it's time for a new lesson, my projects end; Peter's jobs pile up. He calls, and we are back in business again.

Ninety-year-old Ilene Abarr needed a reminder of God's love and truth. She needed to remember the time, eighty years ago, when she attended a church and opened her heart to Jesus. Nobody walks up to Ilene Abarr's home and gets in the door without an extremely important reason. Even if she likes you, it takes time for her to remove the two-by-four out of the iron brackets before opening the door.

Somebody gave her my name after she discovered ants eating her home. What began as an ant and rot repair turned into a complete siding project, a painting job, and a roofing job. I replaced windows, built a fence, trimmed shrubs, mowed the lawn, built a cabinet, enclosed the porch, and rebuilt the pump house. Ilene met my wife and daughters. Through the years they became treasures to her.

Ilene used Neapolitan ice cream to make root beer floats. I drank countless mugs of that exceptional drink while she recounted the highs and lows of her life. All the building projects took a back seat to our relationship. Carpentry was the excuse God used to let my family and me into her heart.

I've often had the privilege to sit at tables with lonely, elderly widows. They call, requesting me to install a dead bolt or repair a door. However, I know the reason for the job: it's a means to cheer up the sorrowful, encourage the downcast, and give confidence to the fearful. Without a useful trade, I'd be a distrusted stranger. With a skill, I become a reliable friend, in a time of need.

When the apostle Paul traveled to Corinth, he teamed up with Jews named Aquila and Priscilla. "And because he was of the same craft, he abode with them, and wrought [worked]: for by their occupation they were tentmakers" (Acts 18:3). God used their common trade of sewing tents to bring these Christians together. I'm confident that God also handpicked their customers, material suppliers, and even their neighboring businesses.

Paul liked to work. "Yea, ye yourselves know, that these hands have ministered unto my necessities, and to them that were with me. I have showed you all things, how that so labouring ye ought to support the weak, and to remember the words of the Lord Jesus, how he said, It is more blessed to give than to receive" (Acts 20:34,35). During seasons of Paul's life, he supported himself and others with a working wage. Yet, his eyes weren't on riches or on a career. He was busy warning every man he met and teaching every man he could, all that he knew about Christ. He had a heart for people everywhere he went, meeting whatever physical and spiritual needs he could.

There's no such thing as a dead-end job, no matter how dull and insignificant it seems to be. When God directs us into a job, it's usually for the people He brings into our lives. He's the One responsible for bringing that obnoxious, tobacco-spitting fellow into the shop. It might be a lesson for us, for him, or more likely for both.

If we only see work as the money we make or the projects we complete, jobs can become a boring waste of time. However, when you understand that employment is a means God uses to put us with people, every job becomes an interesting event and every person a gift.

You already have some talents and skills. As you continue to develop, remember that God plans to use your abilities to provide contacts with people. Customers may need your occupation, but they need what's in your heart even more. They want your encouragement, your perspective on life, and your understanding of God to brighten their way and bring hope. Don't let the cares, riches, and pleasures of your career prevent you from seeing your job as God's doorway to another's heart.

> *The steps of a good man are ordered by the Lord:*
> *and he delighteth in his way.*
>
> (Psalm 37:23)

Questions

- After years of limited communication, what gave Don and me the chance to restore our friendship?

- Ilene Abarr didn't let strangers into her house. Why did she consider letting me in?

- If you believe that jobs are just for earning money and having a career, what do you miss?

- Give two reasons why God handpicks the people we meet in life.

Exit Strategy

In all the trade of war, no feat is
nobler than a brave retreat.

—Samuel Butler

I'd never heard the phrase, "exit strategy," until last fall when Chris described his plans for starting a heating and air-conditioning company. One of his main concerns was how to get out of the business should he decide to quit someday. Months before opening the doors to Innovative Air, Chris developed a plan to gracefully leave the business. He wanted to create a useful company that, in time, could function without him. The day he began the business, Chris began preparing to get out of it.

On commercial airlines, before you ever leave the ground, attendants provide an exit strategy. They tell you how to use your seat for a life jacket if the plane landed on water. In the unlikely event of the plane losing cabin pressure, they show you how to employ oxygen masks. Exit doors are clearly noted and you receive instructions on how to use the evacuation slide. Airline companies want their passengers to know how to get off their planes under all circumstances—before the plane leaves the runway. Most travelers exit by casually walking toward the cockpit and, with a cheery smile and good-bye to the captain, stepping out the door.

Thirty years ago, when I wanted to marry my sweetheart, my thoughts were on building a life together, not on how to get out of the relationship. Wiser men than I knew the importance of considering the end before the beginning. That's why they included, "till death do us part," in the wedding vows.

From the beginning, though I didn't know the term then, I've had an exit strategy for my marriage. It is simple. Either she dies or I die. Faithfully sticking to that plan guides my daily actions. I want to love her, honor her, and cherish her today and every day until death bids us end the union we presently enjoy. Knowing my exit strategy gives me practical wisdom for how I should treat her today.

I used the illustration of marriage because fewer people are taking the time to consider that marriage's only honest conclusion is death. Therefore, they make foolish choices and do things that lead to disaster. Sound marriage partners stick to it for better and worse, for richer and poorer, in sickness and in health until death parts them.

How does all this apply to a job? Don't wait until the last day of work to plan your exit strategy. To finish well, it is good to have the end in sight at the beginning. That vision will direct your actions to your desired goal. If you stopped to consider an exit strategy for your work, you'd surely come up with some ideas like the following:

On the last day of my job,

1) I want to have a record for doing well and always being on time.
2) I want to have the reputation of owning a good attitude.
3) I want to give sufficient notice before I quit so my boss might find and train my replacement.
4) I want to finish all my business. That means returning all tools and owing no debts.
5) I want to be able to look everyone in the eye, knowing I did as much as possible to be at peace with them.

6) I want a heart that desires to see my boss prosper. I want to hear him say as I leave, "Well done. If you ever need a job in the future, come back. We can always use a man like you."

7) When I terminate a position, I want to leave with all my affairs in order so that I might enter my new course with a full heart, a clear conscience, and no regrets.

I've given you only seven off-the-cuff ideas for ending a job well. I'm sure that you could think up better ones, with a little effort, that would make your departure admirable. It's worth your time to consider how you want to finish your current commitments and then keep to your plan. By practicing first-class discharges from jobs and other commitments, you'll develop the wisdom to complete the valuable responsibilities in life.

Someday, if they haven't already, your father and mother will die. How do you want that relationship to end? Is there anything you could do today to improve those relationships so that when the day of parting comes, you end on respectable terms, peacefully, and as much as possible, with all your business completed?

The greatest exit in this life is physical death. No jobs, relationships, or events can compare. Do you have a strategy for this coming grand occasion?

From what I read in the Bible, Jesus Christ, the visible image of our invisible God, came to earth, died, rose from the dead, and returned to heaven that He might provide an exit strategy for us all. He provided the way out of a life of sin into His joyful presence. He also asks us to invite fellow sinners into His joyful fellowship, made available through His exit preparations.

We are all moving toward the end of our lives. What plans do you have that will give you the privilege of hearing God say, "Well done, good and faithful servant, enter into the joy of the Lord"?

May you grasp, at an early age, how to end this temporal life. May that knowledge give you practical wisdom to live, to work, and to prepare for the life to come. May you enter eternity full of joy and by the grace of our Lord Jesus Christ without any debts left to pay. This is a worthy exit strategy.

O that they were wise,
that they understood this, that they would consider
their latter end! (Deuteronomy 32:29)

Questions

- Why should you want to consider exit strategies before starting projects?

- Suppose one of your parents were to die tonight. Is there anything you wish you could do before they left? If so, is it something you could do this very minute?

- Why do airlines give exit strategies before every flight?

- What is God's exit strategy for marriage? How does that help a man know how to live today?

- Do you understand Jesus' plan to exit this life into His eternal joy? Name something you do each day to align with His plan.

Great-Grandpa Cornelius

It is better to trust in work than money; God never buys anything and is forever at work.

—George MacDonald

M r. Cornelius and I met during a father and son camping trip last summer. He fascinated me by his firsthand descriptions of life eighty years ago. Back then, everyone learned to work at a young age. He drove a team of horses when he was only six years old. At six, he possessed a mind for work, an able body, and a purpose within him that pushed him to work. In his day, the wage for driving a team could provide the needs of a family. Therefore, at an age when most children today are starting the first grade, Great-Grandpa Cornelius had the skill and confidence to support a home.

How old are you? Do you have the ability and the drive to support a family? Are you moving in that direction? Or are you, like many boys or young men, still playing every chance you get, letting someone else provide for you? Have you slipped into the thinking that someday you'll earn a living and support a family, but for now there is nothing to do but play sports and computer games?

Things have changed since Great-Grandpa drove horses. Man-sized wages aren't available for six-year-olds. Laws, written to protect children from overwork, now hinder them from working at all. Machines like the automatic bean picker have taken over the manual jobs boys used to find easily.

Though it's harder today to begin earning a living, every diligent boy who starts early, with a purpose, will achieve it. He must face and overcome the thieves that steal his time and the laziness that strips him of his resources.

Amusement is like a robber who captures men. It steals their time. Without time a man can do nothing. Fulfilling your desires for amusement will put you on the road to debt and poverty because it wastes the time God has given to provide for your needs. Recreation is a part of life, but don't be caught playing when it's time for working.

The speed of our world has become a trap for young workers. We think we should make money fast, have jobs that take little effort, and acquire what we need while we do little or nothing. If your father or mother has given you everything, it *has* come fast and easy, and you have done little or nothing. However, that's not a man's world. Usually, a provider must exert effort over time to gain his needs.

A boy should get away from the easy life as quickly as possible. If someone provides your food, shelter, and education, you're a liability. When you were a baby, you had no choice. Others gladly worked for you. However, as you grow, you want to become an asset as soon as possible. A boy desiring to step into the shoes of a provider should begin working as much as possible, today.

A liability takes more than it gives. An asset gives more than it takes. The world is full of young men who are liabilities to their families. They lie around home while their father or mother works. What a shame! May you never be such a waster.

If you want the ability to supply and protect a family someday, begin now to earn your own way. Maybe you are only ten years old and have no money to finance your own meals or pay your rent; still, you could work toward that goal.

Suppose you have two dollars burning a hole in your pocket. You want a treat or a toy. Instead of wasting your money on pleasure, consider buying something useful for your family's dinner tonight. You could possibly afford a can of vegetables, a head of lettuce, or maybe a pound of meat. Those who regularly buy pop or candy might trade that habit for purchasing the ingredients for one meal a week. I can hear a grateful mother telling her neighbor, "My son, Nathan, provided dinner last night. He's developing the vision that will make him a great man."

The neighbor will be shocked and look wishfully over her shoulder to where her son sits in front of the TV, having never imagined such a thing.

It may not seem worth the effort, especially if your parents are wealthy. However, the issue is more than money; it's a matter of vision and purpose. The goal is to develop the fiber of a provider within you. It's using your boyhood wisely that you might enter manhood prepared. Great benefits will come to you and your family when you begin to help your providers by carrying a portion of the load.

If you don't have any money at all, you can still work toward providing your own way by giving your labor. Instead of paying rent money that you don't have, provide maintenance on your home. My nephew Jeremy manages an apartment complex. He trades a large portion of his rent for overseeing the repairs on the building. What labor can you provide to keep your home in good working order?

A small beginning is better than no beginning. A day is coming when you'll sit down to eat in a home where you provide the shelter and food. You'll gratefully look back to when you purposed to begin paying your own way even though you had only pennies to your name.

To pay your way through life, you must earn your way through life. Don't start by trying to earn from your parents or your sister. Learn as soon as possible to get an income. There are times to buy and sell between siblings and parents, but the goal is to bring resources *in* to your home by a service or a product you provide for someone *out*side your home.

As you start, don't worry about how much you make. It's the fact that you are making something that counts. If you gain only five cents by collecting a pop can, it's still a gain. Maybe Mrs. Jones gave you only a quarter for sweeping her porch. If you didn't spend anything that day, your net worth increased.

The goal isn't to get rich. The goal is to learn to be a useful man, not a burden. The apostle Paul said, "Yea, ye yourselves know, that these hands have ministered unto my necessities, and to them that were with me" (Acts 20:34). Paul paid his own way.

Today, my friend Chris started his own commercial air conditioning and heating company, Innovative Air. It's been his goal for years. He wants this business to provide for his family and the families of those who will work with him.

Growing up, Chris didn't have much. His home life forced him to work for his needs. As a boy, he went door to door asking neighbors for something to do. Whatever they needed, he did. Now, as a man, he's a very good worker. The other day, Chris lamented that since he's been preparing for a new business, remodeling his home, and working a regular job, he couldn't find some young man to help with his yard work. "I've never had any boys knock at my door asking for work," he said. "If one ever comes by, I'll hire him!"

Jobs like that are waiting for you. Have you learned to mow a lawn, clean a gutter, or vacuum a car? Can you quickly wash a window without leaving streaks? Are you strong enough to carry boxes from a house into a moving van? Do you know the needs of children? Can you babysit for an hour or two while a parent runs to the store? When a neighbor takes a vacation are you responsible enough to watch their house, walk their dog, and weed their garden?

If you don't know how to accomplish these simple tasks, ask somebody to teach you. Take the time to learn. Every skill you develop becomes a talent to use at home and to serve your neighbors.

The possibilities are endless. Simply find out what people need and provide it. By providing for the needs of others, you'll have the resources to provide for your own.

Last night I talked with Terry, a father of four boys. He said he wanted to teach one of his sons how to wax cars. Most folks feel they should wax their cars more and would gladly pay a skilled worker to do that. They might even set up a regular schedule to have him come every few months.

If you have time to play hours of computer games each week, let's face it: you're a drain on your family's resources and you're losing opportunities to provide for your own home.

It's a tougher day to earn a living than when Great-Grandpa Cornelius drove horses, but it's attainable for every boy who has a vision, a skill, and a drive.

Today is the day to put away your toys and get to work.

When I was a child, I spake as a child,
I understood as a child, I thought as a child:
but when I became a man,
I put away childish things.
(1 Corinthians 13:11)

Questions

- How old was Great-Grandpa Cornelius when he could support a family?

- What are some things that hinder boys from developing into good providers?

- Name some potential jobs a young man could do.

- If you don't have money, what can you do to help provide food and shelter for your family?

- Why did the apostle Paul make tents when he could have been preaching the gospel?

- What can you do today to earn income?

Grudges

*We should be too big to take offense
and too noble to give it.*

—Abraham Lincoln

Peter Wolf and I worked together seasonally for sixteen years. When he is swamped with work, I join him for a few months. When he catches up, I usually go about my own projects while he keeps installing handrails.

There is one other reason that I return to my own jobs. When we irritate each other past the point of endurance, we know it's time to go our separate ways.

I highly respect Peter's abilities and consider it a privilege to work with him. He also thinks highly of me. Most of the time, we enjoy each other's company. But, there are times that our appreciation for each other wanes in the light of our personal quirks. Peter can say and do things that tax my ability to remain civilized. My responses to him make Peter wish I worked somewhere else.

I believe that God brought us together to show how two imperfect men can remain useful friends when they are willing to forgive and overlook each other's faults. Peter says that his poor memory allows him to invite me back to work after the round of disagreements that preceded our last split.

Whatever the reason, we have spent years learning to appreciate the strengths of each other and overlooking many faults. It would have been easy to quit and never attempt to team up again. However, we would miss the benefits that come by forgiving and

enduring. Neither of us has arrived at perfection. Still we are heading that direction.

Just this week we had a small disagreement. In the old days it could have driven us apart for months, or until Peter forgot about how bad it was.

We were installing a curved black-walnut stair rail for our city's Tour of Homes. Tour houses are usually rushed projects. The subcontractors are forced to work as fast as possible to finish on time. A crowd of workers attacked the structure each day: masons, siders, exterior-trim carpenters, interior-trim carpenters, wood-floor layers, countertop installers, and vinyl layers. In the middle of the chaos, Peter and I attempted to concentrate on the staircase.

I was installing very small pieces of trim. Peter walked up and said that he had trouble putting on those parts and wanted them installed with his special glue that burns your brain cells with every breath. I wasn't having a problem using white glue. I couldn't understand his concern. He said that if I didn't want to use his super glue to find something else to do. He would finish it.

It was his staircase and I was the helper. He had every right to do what he wanted, but inside of me a battle began. What I felt like doing then was picking up my tools and going home. I could feel a grudge coming on and I didn't want to stop it.

A grudge is the inward reluctance to give. It's the unwillingness to benefit the people you resent. When you have a grudge against someone you cut them out of your life, even when they are in the same room with you. You don't smile and only talk if absolutely required. A good grudge holder doesn't look at the other person. He refuses to acknowledge their presence. He can be pleasant to everyone else, yet carefully avoid the target of his grudge.

Sometimes husbands hold grudges against their wives. The wife didn't do something he thought she should, or maybe she did something that she shouldn't have. It might be small or large. Another name for a grudge: the cold shoulder. He doesn't talk with her, doesn't smile at her. He may still eat the food she cooks, but acts as if he is alone.

It's hard to maintain a consistent grudge. When his old friend calls on the phone, this husband merrily chats with him for fifteen minutes. As he hangs up, the husband almost turns to tell his wife about what was said, but remembers that he is holding a grudge. He puts on the solemn face and continues his silence.

Grudges require work. Emotionally, you must keep the sour feelings. Mentally, you must remain alert not to smile or look kind. A day of grudge holding is physically exhausting. However, with training, some people are able to maintain an intense grudge for years.

God desires to benefit the world through you. He designed you to be a vessel in which His Spirit grows and bears fruit. He wants to display His mercy, forgiveness, and goodwill everywhere you go. You are like a pipe He wants to use to pour goodness into the world. The only hindrance is that we have the ability to clog our pipes.

Grandpa Dow owns a small older house. Its water pipes developed sludge through the years. Many times I have gone there unsuccessfully attempting to free the lines.

The pipes gathered so much slimy junk on the inside of the walls that only a trickle of tainted water came through. The water stunk and tasted bad. At times chunks sloughed off, clogging the showerhead and toilet valves. Eventually Grandpa had all the pipes replaced. Now his well water flows unhindered to all the fixtures.

Just like those pipes, our hearts can become filled with selfish sludge that blocks the love God wants to funnel through us.

Most of us have the tendency to cut the people we don't like out of our lives. That is why the Sermon on the Mount gives this instruction:

> Ye have heard that it hath been said, Thou shalt love
> thy neighbour, and hate thine enemy. But I say unto
> you, Love your enemies, bless them that curse you, do
> good to them that hate you, and pray for them which
> despitefully use you, and persecute you; That ye may
> be the children of your Father which is in heaven: for
> he maketh his sun to rise on the evil and on the good,
> and sendeth rain on the just and on the unjust. For if
> ye love them which love you, what reward have ye? do
> not even the publicans the same? And if ye salute

your brethren only, what do ye more than others? do
not even the publicans so? Be ye therefore perfect,
even as your Father which is in heaven is perfect.
(Matthew 5:43-48)

Our tendency to avoid people we don't like is contrary to God's
desire to bless the unjust. If we want God to use us, we must let Him
love the unlovely through us. Those who hate and mistreat us are
people God wants to bless through our generous forgiving attitudes, open hearts, and bright smiles. Instead of being sludge-filled
pipes, God wants us to be clear channels, cheerfully blessing the evil
and the good.

When you hold a grudge you think you are punishing the other
person by withholding your wonderful self. "I won't smile at them;
they'll feel the pain; that'll serve them right." But the opposite is
true. Holding a grudge is punishment on *you*. *You* lose the privilege
of delivering God's water of life. *You* stagnate and stink. *You're* the
one emotionally drained. *You* miss God's joy and fellowship.

It is the nature of God to love sinners. They fight and curse
against Him. In return He showers the best on them. If a man
desires to live a Christian life, he must learn to cooperate with God,
to be His pipeline to a fallen race of people.

Peter and I are God's gifts to each other. We have been at odds
countless times, and yet, by God's grace, our friendship continues to
grow. His heart is open to me and mine to him. I can't say that we
won't have our disagreements in the future, but by refusing to hold
grudges, we will continue to bless each other.

God wants to bless the world through you. Let Him clean out
the pipes of your heart that His living water may flow.

Grudge not one against another, brethren, lest ye be
condemned: behold, the judge standeth before the
door. (James 5:9)

Questions

- How is your life like a pipe?

- What is a grudge?

- How does it keep you from being what God created you to be?

- How do you clean sludge from the pipes of your heart?

Increase

If you have great talents, industry will improve them: if you have but moderate abilities, industry will supply their deficiency.

—Joshua Reynolds

My daughter Betsy and I checked out a book from the library on how to build an eight-foot fiberglass boat. With only two sheets of quarter-inch AC plywood, three yards of fiberglass cloth, a gallon of resin, and some paint, the book led us to believe we could make a boat in a weekend. We did finish the boat; however, it took us five months.

As we rowed around the shores of Clear Lake, it amazed us that with only a small amount of materials and some work, we had created a safe and enjoyable way to travel on water. Since neither of us were great swimmers, we appreciated the boat's stability, especially on the 34-degree water.

One of our neighbors, aware of our interest in boats, offered to sell Betsy his eight-foot rowboat rigged for sailing. His price made it more a gift than a sale. She bought it. The boat came with mast, sail, rudder, oars, life jackets, seat cushions, and rope. We liked rowing, but for traveling *up* the McKenzie River behind Leaburg dam, we liked sailing better.

Grandpa then made us a deal. If we replaced his back porch roof, he would give us his canoe. We tore off the old corrugated plastic, rebuilt some of the structure, and applied new clear plastic. We added a beautiful blue aluminum canoe to our fleet, along with life jackets, paddles, outriggers, and ropes.

Betsy and I began building a ten-by-twenty-foot boathouse for all these vessels. We dug six three-foot-deep holes for the six-by-six treated posts we planned to sink into the ground to support the structure. We needed three-quarter crushed quarry rock to pack around the posts so we called Roy Richardson and asked him to deliver a couple of loads.

Roy owns an old orange five-yard dump truck. He came out twice that same afternoon and dumped ten yards of gravel for us to tamp into the postholes and spread level for the floor.

After Roy dumped his loads, we chatted a while. He sat in the seat of his dump truck holding the door open with his foot. I stood on the ground looking up at him. We hadn't seen each other for some time so we caught up on each other's affairs and passed on news about mutual friends. During the conversation, Roy related how, when he's able, he begins the day by going outside and looking up at the stars. He thanks God for all the provisions He has given: health, talents, resources, his dump truck, and backhoe. He knows that God has given him all these things to make increase.

Roy went on to tell me that just that morning a lumberman said he would donate the old Blue River Mill property if it were developed into something useful for kids. Roy could hardly wait to volunteer his backhoe, dump truck, and time to create a running track. "Isn't that why God gives us things like this," Roy asked as he lightly slapped his steering wheel, "to make increase?"

Just like the rest of His creation, God made Roy. Therefore, it is the most natural thing for Roy to make increase every day and enjoy doing it.

In our beehives, a good queen will lay two thousand eggs a day in the spring. Twenty-one days later those eggs have turned into useful working bees. When they begin to feel crowded, half the bees might leave and start a new hive. Increase.

I've watched salmon digging holes on the bottom of Gate Creek. They had returned two hundred miles up the Willamette and McKenzie Rivers to lay thousands of eggs in the stream above the Vida general store.

When Butch Woosley farmed a stretch of land east of Walterville, he relied on the earth's ability to give increase. A pickup load of seed became semi-truck loads of corn. In God's design, everything He creates produces something, "some thirty, and some sixty, and some an hundred" (Mark 4:8). It isn't so much the amount of increase that matters, rather the fact that each part of creation makes increase in proportion to the resources God provides.

God created you too. The world's resources offer themselves for you to gather, to combine with your labor and to make increase. Around here, blackberries hang on the vines free to the pickers in late summer. Firewood waits for a splitter in the fall. Lumber lies in the stacks ready to be cut into furniture or nailed into houses. Stationery rests in the drawer anticipating an author to send letters of encouragement. A great harvest, the souls of men and women, "white and ready," look for laborers. Resources abound waiting for the man who will add himself to them and make increase.

"How was your day?" my wife asks as I come through the door. Many times I have answered, "Great. I got a lot done." Or sometimes, "Oh, not so good. I just couldn't finish anything."

God instilled a desire within each of us to accomplish, create, invent, and build. We tend to feel good when we make increase and not so good when we can't or don't.

Whenever I feel a little discouraged, one thing is sure to perk me up—accomplishing something. I pick some small task like changing the water in the chicken pen. I take on another, like sharpening my chisels. Then another, like cleaning off my desk, or writing that long overdue letter, harvesting some carrots from the garden, washing the truck, or picking up the shop. After a few of these projects life seems to brighten.

Work isn't just a job you are required to do; it's aligning with God to make increase.

Don't sit around bored with life. Look around you. Meager as they might be, find your resources, add to them your labor and make some increase today.

I have planted, Apollos watered; but God gave the increase. So then neither is he that planteth any thing, neither he that watereth; but God that giveth the increase. (1 Corinthians 3:6,7).

Questions

• According to Roy, why has God given him all that he has?

• Where can you see this law of increase in nature?

• What resources do you have?

• What is something you can do to change those resources into increases?

Initiative

Hard work spotlights the character of people: some turn up their sleeves, some turn up their noses, and some don't turn up at all.

—Sam Ewig

et me tell you an imaginary story about a hardworking boy named Go Getter. Go works at the local Fill Me Up gas station. He's never late for work. He shows up exactly on time. At the end of each shift, he accounts for every penny of gas pumped into the cars. Go washes every windshield as he was taught. He cleans the restrooms every two hours precisely according to the schedule.

Mr. Bossman cannot say enough good things about Go Getter. Once when he was talking to the manager of the nearby Grab and Run Grocery, Bossman said, "Go Getter always does *everything* I ask. He never forgets anything. I've never seen an employee like him! He is a dream come true."

In today's working world, Go Getter would be a dream come true. However, as we consider work from a Christian perspective, God would not be impressed. His opinion of Getter is that he is an unprofitable servant. In God's eyes, doing only everything you are commanded to do is the base line, the starting point. Jesus said, "So likewise ye, when ye shall have done all those things which are commanded you, say, We are unprofitable servants: we have done that which was our duty to do" (Luke 17:10).

Our God is not stingy. He doesn't give the bare minimum. He's abundant and overflowing. He's the God of extra miles, the Giver of more than deserved. Therefore, workers that bear His name should offer more than merely obedience. They are alert to their boss's needs and whenever possible provide his wishes before he asks.

One of the best workers I know is my daughter Betsy. We've worked on all kinds of projects together. We built a boat, a house, fences, and porches. We've landscaped and logged. We've cut firewood, repaired the truck, carved out trails, roofed, laid concrete, and installed siding. The reason she is so high on my list of workers is because her help allows me to achieve twice as much as I would alone. Betsy has the ability to stand attentively at my side watching me work. She thinks about what I'm currently doing and what I will do next. She does everything I ask. What makes her shine is that she does more than I ask, even before I think of it.

Betsy plays the initiative game in her mind. She tries to detect what tool I will need next and have it ready for me, even before I know I need it. When I am measuring a board to cut into a rafter, Betsy fetches the Skilsaw. When I turn to look for my saw she is holding it out to me, handle first, just the way I hold it to make a cut. When I prepare to nail a board, if she sees that I left my hammer on the sawhorse, she bounds over and has it. When I reach to my tool pouch for that hammer and it isn't there, she's ready to slap it into my hand the way I need it. Holding the level, the board, the screw, or whatever I need next, and giving it to me right when I need it is as rewarding for Betsy as kicking a soccer goal.

When it's nearly lunchtime on the days when she and I are working at home, Betsy suggests, "Do you want me to go in and make lunch for us?"

"Sure," I reply.

I work until she calls. When I sit down at the table, the meal is ready to eat. After lunch, she cleans up while I go back to work.

Shortly, she is at my side doing what I ask. Inwardly she is playing that game again, of how she can prepare what I need before I ask for it.

This truth does not apply just to jobs. To be great in God's kingdom is to be the servant of all. This means at home, at the neighbors, at Grandma and Grandpa's house, in the classroom, and on the street—wherever you go—look for what needs to be done and do it. A good worker does not act with initiative only when being paid. For him it's a way of life.

Every lesson needs balance. My friend Will noticed when a tree fell in his neighbor's yard. Will has a servant's heart. He's a man of initiative. After some days went by, he thought to himself, "I'll go over while my neighbor is gone to town and surprise him by cutting his tree into useful firewood." When the neighbor came home, he *was* surprised at Will's work.

After thanking him, the neighbor mentioned that his wife had wanted to mill that tree into lumber instead of cutting it for firewood. Oops. When you act with initiative, be sure you are doing what someone wants done.

Many workers try to do as little as possible for the most pay. Bosses understand that and usually have to put up with it. An employer's dream is to find someone like Go Getter, who cheerfully follows all requests.

However, the greatest workers are those exceptional people who do what is expected and, in addition, everything else they can accomplish. The man who obeys God's promptings will give his employer more than he asks and before he asks it. That is God's nature and He displays it through His people.

I hope that you are one of these workers. For in being a profitable worker, you discover a secret that turns work from a boring requirement into an exciting event.

Even as I write this paragraph, my daughter Betsy is waiting for me. As soon as I finish, we'll begin building the stone wall along the road to the creek. I look forward to watching her initiative at work.

And it shall come to pass, that before they call, I will answer; and while they are yet speaking, I will hear. (Isaiah 65:24)

Questions

- Define initiative.

- How does Betsy play the initiative game?

- Why does Go Getter fall short of God's requirements for a profitable servant?

- Imagine one of your jobs. What extra could you do to display initiative?

Maintenance

I wish to preach, not the doctrine of ignoble ease,
but the doctrine of the strenuous life.

—Theodore Roosevelt

My wife likes to make New Year's resolutions. This year she resolved to avoid soft choices. Therefore, she diligently finished the mending pile, made Cuban bread for dinner, and pushed herself to clean the garden house bathroom. When I see her disregard her feelings and choose to work, I want to follow her example.

One thing I don't like about New Year's resolutions: it's easier to make a resolution than to keep it until February.

Like resolutions, it's easier to build a new house than to maintain an older one. Houses are temporary. Our society sees houses as enduring investments and places great merit on getting one of your own. However, a house, a car, or any other possession decays without regular maintenance and repairs. Houses need repainting, reroofing, recaulking, retiling, and replacing of everything from windows to vinyl floors. After building my current house, I don't look forward to rebuilding it again as the materials wear out. Yet I must, if I want to keep a warm, dry place for my family. Building isn't the hard part, maintaining is.

In an effort to avoid soft choices and maintain our home, I accomplished refinishing the wood floors in the kitchen and bathroom this morning. I avoided the job for years because it meant putting the refrigerator and the range in the front room for three days, making a mess with sanding dust, and I lacked the confidence to apply a flawless finish. I finally tackled the project because I knew that without regular maintenance, my house would fall down around me.

Having a few hours of afternoon left after the final coat on the floor, I decided to prune the apple and pear trees. Grabbing my tools, I headed for the orchard. About three hours of work remained to complete this year's trimming. After an hour, I felt like quitting. Besides, today was President's Day.

Not wanting to give in to a soft choice of quitting the moment I felt like it, I made a little bargain with myself, "Keep working until the mailman comes. Then you may quit." I felt confident that the postman would arrive any moment. He was already overdue.

After ten minutes my mind jolted with a thought. *Today's a holiday! There's no mail on holidays!* My no-soft-choices wife walked through the gate about then. I told her about my bargain. She laughed and thought I would surely finish pruning before the mailman arrived tomorrow.

It took the full three hours to finish pruning. It's one thing to dig a hole and plant a tree. It's a different matter to provide the care needed to produce edible fruit on that tree. Planting isn't the hard part, maintaining is.

The slothful man has a roof; however it's covered with moss on the north slope and will soon leak if it doesn't already. The sluggard in Proverbs has a vineyard; it's under a canopy of thorns. He has a stone wall, but it's broken down. The slothful may have a mind to acquire, but he lacks the vision and determination to maintain his goods.

People go through life acquiring things. They think that if they can just get that house or car, they'll be set. Ben Franklin said that it's easier to build two fireplaces than to provide wood for one. A man who cannot see life as an exercise in maintenance collects until he's overrun with things. Then, unless he gets rid of most of it, he spends the rest of his life as a slave attempting to maintain his collections or simply watching them decay around him.

I remember putting together a swing set. The instructions said that I must check each bolt and oil each moving part every two weeks! That's excessive, but it makes a point. If you plan to own things, plan to maintain them. Keep only what you can cheerfully take care of. You'd be better off giving away the stuff you can't sustain to someone who needs it, rather than trying to preserve it for yourself.

Limit your possessions to what you can keep in a reasonable condition. Plan time to enjoy and maintain what you have, before spending time and money to get more.

Examine your possessions. Are they in good working order or broken? It's not that everything must be in perfect condition. I don't want to put a burden upon you that nobody can bear. Though I don't want to burden you, the state of our belongings tends to reflect the state of our hearts. The writer of Proverbs recognizes a sluggard when he looks at the sluggard's fields and fences.

When people visit our homes or walk around our yards, what do they see? Do they see a reasonably cared for house and grounds or do they encounter far more things than a person can maintain, in various degrees of decay? If you can't take care of what you have, consider giving it away to someone who needs it. Acquiring and hoarding goods that you haven't the time or resources to maintain makes a man like a stagnant pool. Like water entering a pool, stuff comes into our lives and piles up. It easily becomes useless and sometimes literally stinks! The man who accepts what comes, takes care of it, or sends it on its way, is like a useful stream that remains clean and provides refreshment for others. What a man acquires doesn't matter much, for goods may come by work, gifts, or just being in the right spot at the right time. What he does with what comes is a test that reveals his outlook on life, goods, and God. The getting isn't hard, the keeping is.

It's easier to:

- Plant a new lawn than keep an established lawn looking sharp.
- Make a marriage vow than to remain married a year.
- Open a checking account than to keep it balanced.
- Ask Jesus to take over your heart than to remain sensitive to Him throughout your life.

We're losing our maintenance mentality in our society partly because of our prosperity. We don't tend to care for items; we throw them away to repurchase new. As we lose the mindset to maintain, we lose an important perspective of our God. He created our world and our hearts with the need for regular maintenance.

The Bible says that Jesus created the world and currently maintains it (Colossians1:15,16). Imagine what it takes to maintain a water system that feeds every living plant and animal on the planet. Think of the challenges to provide continual oxygen, heating, and cooling for a whole world.

He's a maintainer and He created us in His image. Those who accept this role prosper in His kingdom. Those who won't adopt a maintenance mentality, suffer consequences.

As a boy, David prospered while maintaining his father's sheep. Participating in their daily care, he developed the wisdom and skill to lead a kingdom. After becoming king, he failed to give his sons the care they needed. Without timely family maintenance, David's kingdom experienced continual wars all the remaining days of his life.

Paul told Timothy to look for maintenance-minded men as leaders for the church: "One that ruleth well his own house, having his children in subjection with all gravity; For if a man know not how to rule his own house, how shall he take care of the church of God?" (1 Timothy 3:4,5). Rule and maintain are similar words. They both describe keeping something in a particular state, not allowing it to fail or decline. Paul understood that it was easier to give birth to children than to provide the attention required to rear them into self-controlled, useful citizens. Therefore, he set a standard to separate potential leaders from true leaders. If a man could maintain a family over the years, he proved himself as someone that understood God's principles of maintenance. Such a man, when elevated to an office of bishop or overseer, would come with a heart attentive to the daily needs of those under his care. These men are pictures of God's heart and provide an example for all Christian men to follow.

Whether you consider a business, a home, or a fruit tree, each will fall like the sluggard's rock wall without regular maintenance.

Don't be so interested in acquiring something more or new that you miss taking care of what you have. It's costly to buy a new car when only a few quarts of oil could have saved the engine of your old one. Every mechanic can tell you of engines that could have avoided destruction if the owner had taken a minute to check the dipstick.

Acquiring is easy. Maintaining is the challenge. May God place within you the vision and drive to take care of what He has given to you, before you long for something new.

Keep thy heart with all diligence; for out of it are the issues of life. (Proverbs 4:23)

Questions

- What does the word *maintain* mean?

- Why is maintaining something harder than getting something new?

- Why does Paul make maintaining a family a qualification for leadership in the Church?

- What does it mean to "keep your heart with all diligence"?

P.S. While I wrote this chapter, my neighbor Jonathan came over to help me with my bees. He's a diligent beekeeper who gives regular attention to his hives. His experienced eye detected American Foul

Brood on my frames of brood. I should have spotted that disease long before.

The only sure remedy to protect my neighbor's bees from this disease was to burn my equipment. Pinewood and beeswax makes for a hot bonfire! I lost hundreds of dollars of equipment and put the neighborhood hives at risk because I failed to give my bees regular maintenance.

Also, when my friend George came for dinner this week he told me that twice he has failed to check the oil in his cars and burned up the engines as a result.

I hope you can learn about maintenance by hearing stories like these instead of paying expensive consequences yourself.

Have you ever lost something because you failed to take care of it?

Me Own Dog Tucker

"It is a great blessing to possess what one wishes,"
said one to an ancient philosopher, who replied,
"It is a greater blessing still, not to desire what one
does not possess."

—Wm. M. Thayer

My wife's dog was a Welsh Corgi she officially named, "Me Own Dog Tucker." He had a slender nose and pointed ears much like a fox. Bred for herding cattle, he resembled a small barrel, able to roll with a hoof kick. People often laughed the first time they saw him because his stocky legs were so short they did look strange.

Tucker was smart. I trained him how to stay on third base until he got the signal to run for home. He learned to slide into the plate with a roll to avoid the tag of a catcher. That dog could say, "HHHoooowww are ya," as he greeted me in the mornings. When he killed seven moles one year, Tucker gained my admiration as a useful contributor to the family cause.

I've heard the term "greedy dogs" before, but Tucker brought new meaning to those words. My daughter liked to hold a bit of food between her fingers and watch him rivet his eyes onto that morsel. He'd sit motionless, with every muscle tense like a snake, ready to strike. Then the drool began to flow in one or two streams from his lips to the ground. Nothing in the world mattered any more except gaining the object of his desire.

Sometimes Tucker would sneak away at night. In the morning his bloated stomach and unquenchable thirst betrayed this wayfarer. His undersized legs, which hardly kept his chest off the ground when he was empty, couldn't keep his belly off the lawn.

Once we got a grand idea to help him over his love affair with food. We placed an open bag of dog food on the porch and planned to let him eat whatever he wanted. Surely he would fill up and quit eating. I've seen some golden retrievers and a few border collies eat reasonably with this arrangement. Poor Tucker, he began eating feverishly and didn't quit until he couldn't swallow another bite. Half sitting and half lying down, for he couldn't do either very well, he stared at the food bag, moaning and burping.

The dog's greedy appetite contributed to his untimely end. He ate something that turned cement-like in his large intestines. The veterinarian tried to save him, but alas, Tucker's keen desire for anything that resembled food killed him. Greed is a hungry desire for some object or goal that you don't possess. For Tucker it was anything edible. Food was essential to keep that dog alive but when it became his focus, it turned into greed. When a desire becomes the center of our attention at the exclusion of other useful and responsible thoughts, we're greedy.

Greed is a serious matter. It prevents a man from enjoying what he already possesses and leaves him discontented. Greed blinds a man's understanding. The worst consequence is that a greedy man loses his awareness of God's presence.

Suppose Joe has a computer. For over a year he's enjoyed the efficient work he's accomplished on it. Last week Joe visited Danny. Danny had a new computer that was four times faster than his. Now every time Joe sits down at *his* computer he thinks about *Danny's* computer. The tendency to focus on what we don't possess prevents us from enjoying what we do.

Understanding is the ability to see how little things fit into the bigger picture of life. By focusing intently on only one thing, a man loses his ability to see how that object relates to other areas of life.

Stephen stood at the fence, staring at the delicious apple tree in Mr. Connelly's yard. His understanding began to fade. The thought of juicy fruit sliding down his dry throat blinded him to the dog lying under the bush near the house. He also couldn't visualize the look on his father's face when he heard that his son was caught stealing. Greed blinds our understanding.

Imagine...It's the last afternoon of hunting season. While spotting through his scope, Gomer spies a scraggly spike swallowing succulent shrubbery. Moving his gun until the cross-hairs center on a sure kill, he senses a little disappointment that this youngster should become his fall harvest. However, that's all he's seen and it's probably his last chance for any meat.

After the well-placed shot, he lowers his scope. A movement catches his eye on the right. Jerking his head toward it, Gomer sees a large, five-point buck bound into the trees.

That's how greed works. Intently focused on something in the distance, we become blind to what is nearby. If Gomer would have removed his eye from the limited scope for a moment and looked around, he might have seen an option he didn't know existed. Greed darkens a man's understanding.

One evening King David focused on a woman named Bathsheba. If he had put down his scope and looked around him, he might have enjoyed a walk with his wife Abigail. But no, he kept his focus on a wife he didn't have. David's one-track mind led him away from the path of understanding and wisdom, into the path of stealing, lying, and murder. His coveting heart removed him from the joy of God's presence. When David came back to his senses, he begged God, in Psalm 51, not to cast him away from His presence but to restore the joy of his salvation. Of all the harm greed brings to a man, the loss of sensing God's presence is the worst.

Greed always thinks that the grass is greener on the other side of the fence. The greedy man doesn't enjoy what he already owns, because his heart is on things just out of his reach.

For many folks, life is a rat race. That means they race after something in the distance, trying to get there before any other rats arrive. When they achieve that car, house, wife, career, or other object they've been chasing, they pause only long enough to put it into their shopping cart before zooming on to get something more. Rat-race runners live discontentedly, without understanding and without the secure pleasure of God's presence.

I find myself entering this race when I focus on the next job before finishing the one at hand. With my eyes on the next project I don't stop to put away the tools and materials from building bee

hive equipment before sitting down at my desk to write. Then I jump up from writing. Leaving my papers and books scattered, I focus on the sunshine and my need to get a dormant spray on the apple trees before the buds open.

I can tell, and so can my family, when I'm falling into a greedy mindset. My shop, truck, and office become a mess. Instead of fully enjoying and finishing my jobs, my eyes are two steps ahead on the rat-race road.

When I catch myself gulping food in anticipation of dessert, I'm aware of my greed. If I relaxed and enjoyed the great meal in front of me, I might not even want a treat. I'd be full of good things.

It's sad to watch a man who once enjoyed walking in God's presence give himself to greed. He stops appreciating God and focuses on some item he doesn't have. Though he may not slobber like Tucker, his actions show that he disregards all else in life while staring at what he doesn't possess.

God didn't make us to live like dogs. We don't have to give in to greed. It's your choice. Do you want to be a self-controlled man or a drooling dog?

I know what God wants to give you. It's a contented heart, full of understanding and joyfully aware of His presence. May His desire be yours today.

His watchmen are blind: they are all ignorant, they are all dumb dogs, they cannot bark; sleeping, lying down, loving to slumber. Yea, they are greedy dogs which can never have enough, and they are shepherds that cannot understand: they all look to their own way, every one for his gain, from his quarter. Come ye, say they, I will fetch wine, and we will fill ourselves with strong drink; and to morrow shall be as this day, and much more abundant. (Isaiah 56:10-12)

Questions

- Why did Tucker die an early death?

- What is greed?

- Name three consequences that come upon a greedy man.

- Of the three, which is the worst? Why?

- How can greed lead to a messy shop? Bedroom?

This chapter exposes some of our greed and its consequences. The following chapter will describe a simple remedy.

Transported with Delight

*Happiness is a thing to be
practiced, like the violin.*

—John Lubbock

Have you ever looked upon a baby as he finished nursing? Have you seen an infant so full that he couldn't suck once more? His head gently falls back displaying a face lost in ecstasy. Red cheeks, wet to the neck with overflowing warm milk, eyes rolled back into his eyelids, a sleepy smile—every muscle in his body limp with fulfillment.

If you've never seen a baby like that, I wish you could. I also wish you could keep that picture in your mind always, because the antidote for a greedy heart is to thankfully enjoy your food. How simple can it get?

"Your breakfast is ready," my wife called this morning. Approaching the table, I saw half a grapefruit sitting on my plate. I couldn't remember the last time I ate a grapefruit. Looking forward to scrambled eggs and toast, my first thought was, "I don't like grapefruit." My second thought was, "You're greedy. You're wanting what you don't have. Enjoy the food on your plate."

Honestly, how can I encourage you to enjoy what you eat while I complain about my food? We sat down and thanked God for our meal, and though a bit unusual in my taste world, that grapefruit was quite good! Not only did I enjoy the breakfast, I enjoyed my wife and most of all, my God, who turned my greedy thought into grateful joy.

Many times I've failed to delight in what was before me because I longed for something else. When I complain, I rob myself, and everyone around me, of that moment's pleasure.

The nation of Israel had the same problem. Deuteronomy 6:10-12 says, "And it shall be, when the LORD thy God shall have brought thee into the land which he sware unto thy fathers, to Abraham, to Isaac, and to Jacob, to give thee great and goodly cities, which thou buildedst not, And houses full of all good things, which thou filledst not, and wells digged, which thou diggedst not, vineyards and olive trees, which thou plantedst not; when thou shalt have eaten and be full; Then beware lest thou forget the LORD, which brought thee forth out of the land of Egypt, from the house of bondage."

God gave His people enough to keep them all content. He wanted them to eat until they fell back like satisfied babies. For He said, "When thou hast eaten and art full, then thou shalt bless the LORD thy God for the good land which he hath given thee" (Deuteronomy 8:10).

Instead, Israel looked up from their abundant tables, looked out the windows of their secure homes, stood at their cool wells, and turned their eyes to see how the Hittites, Amorites, and Canaanites worshipped their gods.

How tough is it to thankfully enjoy what God has given? The Israelites refused. Instead, they began worshiping goats, golden statues, and even burned their children to satisfy false gods.

False gods originate in the minds of men. Without an understanding of true goodness, they imagine harsh and cruel beings that expect men to save themselves through sacrifices and self-inflicted suffering.

Our God is different. He's alive and not imaginary. His methods and morals are far higher than we can think, and He is good.

In the beginning, He created a garden for Adam. "And out of the ground made the LORD God to grow every tree that is pleasant to the sight, and good for food; the tree of life also in the midst of the garden, and the tree of knowledge of good and evil…And the LORD God commanded the man, saying, Of every tree of the garden thou mayest freely eat: But of the tree of the knowledge of

good and evil, thou shalt not eat of it: for in the day that thou eat-est thereof thou shalt surely die" (Genesis 2:9,16,17).

At the start, God delighted Adam and Eve with His plants, ani-mals, and every good thing. He filled their senses with happiness. Their greatest joy was His presence.

God gave abundantly with one small limitation: Don't eat from the tree of the knowledge of good and evil. This request set up the first recorded example of greed. With unlimited food at their fin-gertips, Eve stared at the forbidden fruit. Her discontentment grew. She wanted what she didn't have. Almost without her knowing it, her wayward desire drew her from the joy of God's presence. She disobeyed, ate, and then purposely hid from her Creator.

A secret to worshipping God is to forget what you can't have and thankfully find pleasure in what you do have. Adam could have said, "Eve, this tree isn't for us. Come with me. Have you ever tasted blueberries like these? Sit in this grassy spot. Feel the warm sun. Rest here and smell the fragrances. Try this juicy berry. I'll get the biggest ones I can find and feed them to you. Eve, don't we have a wonderful God Who has given us all things richly to enjoy!"

Life for Adam and Eve would have been different had they thankfully delighted in the food God gave them.

How does this apply to work and business?

Many men strive for a bigger business, a newer truck, and bet-ter conditions. If we would worship God by thankfully savoring the positions and goods we have, we would be full of joy now, instead of longing for it in the future.

My father-in-law practiced dentistry. He stayed on the leading edge of products and procedures by attending seminars. At some seminars, the wisdom of the day encouraged him to build a bigger building, hire more hygienists, and even another dentist. Thinking that advice to be true, he followed it.

The stress of accepting the world's wisdom cost him his health. If he could do it over again, he would seriously consider enjoying what he already had. He says a wiser move would have been to make an office in his garage and with one trustworthy assistant, provide quality dental care for a small number of patients. He thinks he would have enjoyed his practice more in a converted garage than in the dental complex he acquired.

The goal isn't necessarily to be small. The size of your business, your production, or even your influence matters little. The goal is to possess a heart that delights in God. A man reaches this end when he accepts what he has, whether little or great, as gifts from God. Delightful thanksgiving is the beginning of worshipping our Creator in spirit and truth.

Have you ever tried putting a bite of food in your mouth then laying down your fork and not picking it up again until your mouth is empty? That's a challenge for me. Often, there is another full fork waiting in the air before I finish chewing the first. When I catch myself eating like that, it's a reminder I'm not enjoying what I have. I'm greedily longing for more.

At first glance, encouraging someone to enjoy every bite of their food may seem sensual. I'm suggesting that you take one bite and enjoy it thoroughly, before taking another and doing the same. Enjoying to the limit one teaspoon at a time will tend to keep you from overeating.

Thankful enjoyment of God's gifts is one remedy against the lust of the flesh, the lust of the eyes, and the pride of life. Whether it's food, clothes, your home, or your business, may you learn to take pleasure in what you have and thereby live thankful, contented, and joyful in your Father's presence.

Charge them that are rich in this world,
that they be not highminded, nor trust in uncer-
tain riches, but in the living God,
who giveth us richly all things to enjoy.
(1 Timothy 6:17)

Questions

- A review question from the last chapter: What is greed?

- What does the word *antidote* mean?

- What is an antidote for greed?

- Why did Israel follow false gods?

- What is something you could choose to enjoy today that you normally don't?

How Could It Be My Fault?

A man should never be ashamed to own he has been
in the wrong, which is but saying, in other words,
that he is wiser today than he was yesterday.

—Alexander Pope

Hello, Will? This is Bob. I have a few days off from building handrails. May I come out in the woods and run the skidder for you?"

"Sure, I'll pick you up tomorrow morning on my way by."

Will was logging alone and welcomed the request. He fell and bucked the trees. I yarded the logs to a landing where a self-loading log truck picked them up.

At the end of one day, the truck driver said, "The road is getting pretty slick. I think I can make it out, but listen for me." Will and I stood quietly on the landing listening to the rumble of the truck pulling up the slippery grade.

The engine quieted down.

"I think he's stuck," Will said.

Will walked to the skidder. I began running up the road. After a hundred yards, I saw the truck going out of sight around a curve.

Will caught up to me with the skidder and said, "It looks like he made it. Hop on. I'll give you a ride back."

Skidders are machines designed to drag logs out of the brush. They drive over almost anything that gets in their way. Sometimes they remind me of a carnival ride. The driver straps himself inside a wire protection cage. Moving through the woods, he's jolted and jerked around like a pop machine when an big angry guy puts his money in and no pop comes out. Can you imagine it?

This skidder runs on four rubber tires, each about six feet tall. It articulates in the center. That means that the tires do not steer like a car; instead the whole machine has a hinge in the middle. In a full turn, the front tires almost touch the back tires. Between these tires is a small step the operator uses to climb up into the driver's cage. Any riders must stand on that step between the two tires. You hope that you have an operator who knows what he is doing, and who has your interests in mind if you accept a ride.

Will is that sort of man. He's always careful with me around the equipment. He likes to see me go home alive each night almost as much as I do.

Looking over his left shoulder, Will began backing up. I stood on his right side looking at those big tires slowly revolving only twelve inches from my boots. I put one foot up on the floorboard near Will's feet and hugged the cage.

About then the diesel engine screamed and Will sped up. Those big tires began bouncing and swaying as Will raced that skidder backwards down the narrow, rough road. I couldn't believe it was happening. One slip and I was dead.

I wanted to jump off, but that was surely suicide. He yelled something about getting my foot up. My one leg still dangerously threaded the space between the wheels. I couldn't pull myself into the cab. I felt like an bug inside a cassette tape that had just been turned to fast forward. I could hear Will yelling something, but the skidder yelled louder. I wanted to scream, "Let me off of here!" However, nothing came out of my mouth!

Once Will blindly swung his fist. He hit me and almost knocked my leg out of the cab. I hung on tighter. Why did I climb on here in the first place? I thought. What has gotten into Will? *Helllllp!*

In desperation, while still looking back over his left shoulder, Will swung a backhanded right fist. He hit my leg hard enough to knock my foot out of the cage…and off the accelerator.

The skidder abruptly stopped.

I jumped to the ground. Our eyes met. I felt stupid. Both of us could hardly believe what had just happened.

I told him that I'd walk the rest of the way.

He thought that was a good idea.

When the skidder began screaming, Will thought the throttle had stuck. It had happened to him once before. Then he realized that my boot had the fuel pedal pinned to the floorboard! The challenge of looking over his shoulder while driving top speed backwards down a narrow logging road kept him too busy to get me out of the cab. Pumping the brakes didn't help. He couldn't yell loudly enough for me to hear him. In desperation, his blind slam hit my leg. He saved me from a terrible accident.

Later, Will related, "This would be hard to explain to the insurance man: he ran over himself while I was driving!"

From my perspective, Will was about to kill me! He drove recklessly, without any regard for my safety. My whole future rode in the hands of a man who had gone crazy. I had no doubt that he was completely at fault.

Will's twenty-two years of experience with that machine saved me from my own foolishness.

I hope you never ride on a runaway skidder. However, I'm sure you will face similar situations. Maybe it will be an out-of-control boss screaming at you. You may have an irate customer to deal with. Perhaps just today you've had a quarrel with a brother or sister. Any argument or confrontation could turn out as wild as my ride with Will. When life gets out of hand that's the time to stop and consider, "Is this problem my fault?"

"The way of a fool is right in his own eyes" (Proverbs 12:15). We have the tendency to see the faults of others before considering our own shortcomings. Convinced of our right standing, we are blind to the fact that we might be part or even the whole problem.

God understands we are a big part of the troubles we face in life. In Proverbs He words the same idea three more ways, trying to catch our attention, "All the ways of a man are clean in his own eyes; but the LORD weigheth the spirits" (16:2). "Every way of a man is right in his own eyes: but the LORD pondereth the hearts" (12:15). And, "There is a generation that are pure in their own eyes, and yet is not washed from their filthiness" (30:12).

A blind spot is some flaw in our character, or speech or actions that everyone else sees but we cannot. For me, my blind spot was my foot on the accelerator. Will saw it. He had a good reason for swinging his fist at me, though I couldn't understand why at the time.

Imagine this: Joe walks up to the waitress at the club house and asks about the lunch special. He's wearing his new golf shoes. The waitress always wears sandals. Joe accidentally gets too close. He doesn't mean to, but he stands on her foot. While Joe chats, her face begins turning red. Then, without warning, she hauls off and slaps him hard enough to send him into the nearest booth. She turns and hops on one foot, back into the kitchen. Joe shakes his head and says to himself, "I wonder what got into her." Joe has a blind spot.

You and I have blind spots like Joe. What are mine? I don't know. If I knew, it wouldn't be my blind spot. Knowing we have blind spots should cause us to be a little less self-confident. Maybe we're not all right and maybe everybody else isn't all wrong. It ought to make us stop and consider our ways.

Probably somebody has tried to tell us about our blind spots already, but we didn't believe them. Maybe we just figured they had a problem and were blaming us for it.

The next time you have a disagreement with somebody, or perhaps have some other trouble on your hands, pause and ask yourself, "Am I part of this problem?"

If you have the courage, though not many men do, try going a step further. Ask the person opposite you, "Do you think I have a blind spot that is causing trouble between us?" You might be surprised to hear what they say.

It's the godly man who looks for his own foot before he criticizes somebody else.

Who can understand his errors?
cleanse thou me from secret faults.
(Psalms 19:12)

Questions

- I thought that the runaway skidder was Will's problem. Was I right?

- Whose fault was it?

- What's a blind spot?

- What should you ask yourself next time you're in trouble?

My Instructor

Quiet waiting before God would save from many a mistake and from many a sorrow.

—J. Hudson Taylor

At two o'clock in the morning, I couldn't sleep. It was useless to try anymore. I got up, went to the front room, threw a log into the woodstove and stared at the flames.

In a few hours my boss expected me to begin the interior woodwork on a new house. Not just any new house, but the biggest and fanciest house I'd ever built. The foundation was easy enough. We got through the framing O.K. However, now he wanted me to install the trim and I had only a little experience.

Thinking of the massive entry staircase, the expensive walnut paneling for the living room, the truckload of tongue-and-groove cedar for the library left me weak with fear. I'd never nailed on one piece of baseboard before, let alone all this costly wood. How could I do anything but fail?

I poured out my heart to God telling Him my fears and worries. My spirit calmed but my stomach remained in a knot. From two until six o'clock I read the Bible, listening for His answer to my need.

Sometime around six He spoke to my heart, "Don't you think that I, who built the world, know how to build a house? I know how to put on paneling. I know how to build staircases. And, I know how to tell you how to do it."

The question for me wasn't whether He knew how, but could He communicate it to me? How would *He* teach *me* to install paneling?

He continued speaking to me, "Didn't I tell Moses *exactly* how to build the tabernacle? Didn't I show Solomon *exactly* how to build the temple? Didn't I tell Noah *exactly* how to build the ark? You don't need to know how to build stair rails tonight. When the day comes I will tell you. Diligently do what you already know. I will tell you what you need to know when you need it."

By the time the sun came up, God had calmed my fears. He promised His wisdom and convinced me that He would communicate it. I wasn't overflowing with boldness that morning, but I did have the courage to show up for work. He was there and He kept His word.

I stood in the living room holding the first sheet of paneling. A painter walked through the door beside me. "Hey," he said, "I saw a carpenter once putting on some of that paneling and he…" At that point the painter began to speak as if he was lecturing to a classroom of new paneling installers. After telling me everything I needed to know, he apologized, "I don't know why I told you all that, I'm sure you know it already." Embarrassed by his outburst of information, he ducked from the room.

I followed God's advice given to me through the painter. The paneled walls turned out beautifully. No one would imagine that the installer began without knowing how.

My God taught me how to build stairs. I blundered my way into the double valutes, upeasings, and newels. With His help, I precisely installed the parts. The verse from James 1 became a living truth. "If any of you lack wisdom; let him ask of God, that giveth to all men liberally, and upbraideth not; and it shall be given him." Throughout the job, God brought to my mind just what I needed to know to finish the house and to exceed my boss's expectations.

Twenty-five years later God still instructs me. He isn't a distant God, uninvolved in the lives of His people. He continually offers all I need to live and work wisely, if I will just listen.

Proverbs 8:1-6 says,

> Doth not wisdom cry? and understanding put forth her voice? She standeth in the top of high places, by the way in the places of the paths. She crieth at the gates, at the entry of the city, at the coming in at the doors. Unto you, O men, I call; and my voice is to the sons of man. O ye simple, understand wisdom: and, ye fools, be ye of an understanding heart. Hear; for I will speak of excellent things; and the opening of my lips shall be right things.

The wisdom of God is out in the work places, the streets, and the businesses. His voice cries to men, proclaiming how to live. His wisdom is not confined to church meetings and Bible studies. His wisdom and voice are not limited to the religious. God's wisdom constantly speaks even for the benefit of fools and simple folks, people like you and me.

Just yesterday, as I trimmed three arched windows in a fire-engine red dining room, the tile setters entered a hall behind me. One of them lamented, "We need a light to work in the utility room. This morning I thought about getting a light, but I didn't put it in the truck."

Who do you suppose put it in their mind to take a light? I believe God tried giving them wisdom. On that occasion they didn't listen.

Were the tile setters Christians? I don't know and it doesn't matter when it comes to hearing the wisdom of God. God sends rain on the just and the unjust. He gives wisdom to any who will listen. The question isn't, "Does God speak?" The question is, "Will we listen?"

"I will instruct thee and teach thee in the way which thou shalt go: I will guide thee with mine eye," says the Lord in Psalm 32:8.

If you want to be a good worker, develop the ability to hear God's voice, and have a heart ready to obey what you hear. There are times as I walk to my truck in the morning the thought comes to my mind,

"Take your ladder."

"What could I need my ladder for today?" I think to myself.

"You just might want to take it."

Later in the day I find myself needing a ladder. If I've responded to the voice of wisdom, I have the ladder. If I've rejected wisdom, I might find myself standing on a five-gallon bucket on top of a chair, trying to install a piece of crown molding.

When you are walking out the door and you have the thought, "Take your coat today," grab your coat before you leave.

"But, it's sunny today," you reply.

God will not force you. Maybe He knows something you don't and He would like you to prepare for it ahead of time.

Work is not one day of drudgery after another. It is a moment-by-moment experience with the Creator of the universe. He designs tasks and then tells us the best way to accomplish them. Listening to His voice and doing what He says is the foundation of an abundant life experience, no matter what your occupation may be.

God loves to speak, to teach, and to lead. He constantly teaches anyone willing to learn. A good worker will listen for God's practical instructions and follow them. I hope that describes you. If it doesn't, start today to pay attention to the wisdom God is speaking to you. Your God isn't a distant being who left the world to fend for itself. He's constantly speaking. May you have the ears to hear.

> *My sheep hear my voice, and I know them, and they follow me.* (John 10:27)

Questions

- Who, in the Bible, did God teach how to build?

- How did God give me the wisdom to install four-by-eight sheets of paneling?

- Why do you like to give wisdom to people around you?

- Do you have any examples of when you needed wisdom and God gave it to you?

Plodding

Obstacles are the glory of life.

—Anonymous

In the early seventies, I installed foundations and framed houses for Kas Braun. He employed three four-man crews. Ron Flammang supervised one of those crews. At thirty-five, Ron seemed like an old man from my twenty-three-year-old perspective. I learned a lot from Ron, but what I remember most was a lesson he showed me one rainy winter morning.

The clock read 6:55. Ron and I sat in his old Ford pickup waiting to start work at seven. It was a day we wished we could do something besides work. Steam from Ron's coffee added to the already foggy windshield. We rolled down the side windows about an inch to let in some fresh air and to give us a better view of the rain and the dreary job site.

I didn't have the financial responsibilities Ron had. I could miss a day of work without feeling pressure. I didn't want to work in the rain, yet I didn't want to look too eager to go home either.

Excuses abound for not working in the rain. Rusty tools, slippery hammers, gummed up chalk lines, and soaked T-shirts are just a few of them.

"How about it, Ron?" I asked. "Do you think we should go home? We won't get much done here today even if we do try to work."

Ron knew all the excuses too. And being older he probably had a few more I hadn't even thought about. However, in Oregon, if you don't work in the rain you don't work very often. Ron was in a tough spot. He knew that if he didn't work, his family didn't eat. He also knew that if he announced that we were working all day, his crew would revolt.

"Since we're already here," he bargained, "let's work until 10:00. The crew won't get as much done as usual. We'll just plod along and see if the weather changes."

He was the boss. We bailed out of the truck into the rain and started stretching out electric cords and air hoses. Ron used his rain pencil that wrote like ink on wet wood. He laid out walls and made cutting lists. The rest of us carried lumber and pounded nails.

When we first started working on dark and wet mornings, we were cold. However, before long, our T-shirts began acting like wet suits, providing some comfort. The guys who had a good set of rain gear had an advantage for the first half an hour. If they stood around, the rain gear kept them dry. However, once they began working hard, the pants and coats held in their sweat about as well as they kept out the rain. Either way, within the hour the whole crew was soaked to the skin.

At 10:00, we took a break. The rain hadn't changed much. We had a few walls up. Not a great showing for the morning's work but better than if we had gone home.

Ron made a new suggestion. "It's less than two hours until lunch. Let's work until then. I know that the mud is making things slippery. Take your time, plod along and see what we can do. In a couple of hours, we'll have half a day in and then we can go home, if the weather doesn't improve."

At noon the weather improved. I was afraid of that. I still secretly hoped to go home. I didn't have anything special to do, but once a young man gets it in his mind that he might have the day off, it's hard to change his direction.

With the weather slightly improving, after lunch Ron suggested that we work until 2:30. By then the sun was shining. How could I justify going home early from work on a sunny day?

Instead of avoiding work at the thought of facing an uncomfortable day, Ron had the vision of setting a small goal and completing what we could. We started that morning with just the floor of the house laid. By four o'clock, we had the outside walls standing. Everyone knew that we usually accomplished much more in a day. However, without Ron's leadership we wouldn't have accomplished anything. We went home as conquerors instead of quitters.

Wouldn't it be great to wake up every morning feeling completely rested with all of your muscles in tip-top shape and free from all injuries? To have before you only one project to accomplish and all the materials you need stacked ready for use? To have the temperature a balmy 70 degrees with a slight breeze? To have the wisdom and skill to accomplish your task and to find everything falling into place so that you finish all you dreamed and even more?

That would be great; however, life is rarely that way. Often a slight hindrance keeps us from being able to work at peak efficiency. That is no excuse for not doing what we can. The man who waits for perfect conditions before he starts his projects will never start anything and therefore never finish anything. On the contrary, the man who begins today, even when he knows it will be a small beginning, will find a completed project at the end of his efforts.

It's been many years since I watched Ron Flammang plod along. He finished house after house, on rainy days, on hot days, and even on days when he felt sick. Ron worked fast when he could. He worked slower when he had to, but he never quit.

Ron's example has encouraged me to keep going, even if the pace is slow. It's amazing how many projects I complete while plodding along on dreary, wet days.

The sluggard will not plow by reason of the cold;
therefore shall he beg in harvest,
and have nothing. (Proverbs 20:4)

Questions

- Why did Ron want to work on a dark and rainy day?

- What was his plan for getting the rest of us to work?

- What is wrong with waiting for the perfect circumstances before beginning to work?

- At the end of the day, would you rather be a quitter or a conqueror?

The Plumbline

Important principles may, and must be, inflexible.

—Abraham Lincoln

His real name was Paul. We called him *Herfy*. We named him after a Herfy's Hamburger Restaurant. Their sign displayed a cartoon picture of a Hereford bull. Paul and that bull looked a lot alike.

Our Herfy ran a four-man crew installing foundations and framing houses. He weighed about two hundred and thirty pounds—all muscle.

I knew of his muscles because we wrestled almost every day. After lunch somebody would start it by a shove, a pinch, or by kicking a lunch bucket. Soon it was a free for all, dog piles, fireman carries, head locks. Arms and legs flailed in the air. Herfy liked having everyone wrestling at once, especially if all of us were against him.

I weighed only 155 pounds, which was no match for Herfy. However, I gained his respect by my continual efforts to take him off his feet and for enduring his power crunches and painful belly pinching. I needed Herfy's respect; it gained me a place under his care. When I got in a jam while wrestling other crewmembers, Herfy was always close by, ready to pinch or twist my opponent's leg.

Herfy taught me how to wrestle; he also taught me how to build.

The first morning I arrived on the job, Herfy set me straight about building houses. The foundation stood ready for us framers. Piles of lumber and plywood littered the driveway. The sun peeped over the Coburg hills preparing to melt the light layer of frost. With a framing square in hand, he gave me a lecture. I don't remember the particulars but thirty years later I still remember his main point, "Build plumb and square and you'll stay out of trouble."

Plumb means straight up and down. Our world has one clearly defined standard for what's plumb and you don't need a sophisticated machine to determine it.

Anyone can easily make an accurate instrument to determine a vertical line. Tie a rock or any other weighty object to the end of a string and let it dangle like a yo-yo. The string stretches out straight. When it stops swinging you have a plumb line.

Though there's nothing more accurate than a string with an attached weight, I do own a pack of expensive spirit levels, and I did purchase a laser level two summers ago. They're handy and quickly give me the information I need. Plus, they don't swing around when the wind blows. However, I can't always trust them. They need regular checkups to make sure they haven't lost their sense of level and plumb. My eight-foot Stabilia level caused me some serious problems before I realized it was lying to me. I had to get a new one that would line up with my string and plumb bob.

Plumb is simple to determine. However, aligning everything you build to a plumb line can be more difficult than wrestling with Herfy. Crooked lumber, making a cutting error, or not paying attention to the dip of a foundation can put house walls and floors out of level. When the walls lean, doors don't close properly and pictures hang crooked.

If you're someone who looks on the bright side, you might enjoy a house where dropped marbles all roll to the corner so you can pick them up easily. However, most folks don't appreciate that quality in the new home they are about to purchase. Good builders pay attention to their houses and have the skills to begin their projects level and plumb and to keep them that way until the end.

Knowing what's plumb is essential in building. It's also important in other jobs. My friends Gary and Will are loggers. Before they fall a tree they need to know which way it leans. A misjudgment can cost hundreds of dollars when the tree falls in an unplanned direction. I remember when one logger fell a tree on the corner of his Izusu Trooper and the time another laid one into bare power lines. Every faller can tell you stories of trees that seemed to lean one way—but fell another.

That's why Will and Gary use a line to determine the lean of a questionable tree before falling it. When they need a plumb line,

they'll make one from the junk they might find in the back of their truck. An old spark plug and a piece of fishing line will do.

In the woods, when the ground looks flat but actually slopes gently, and all the trees lean in one direction, a tree may look like a leaner when it's not. Holding up their line and comparing the tree to it provides valuable information they need to bring it down safely.

Knowing what's plumb is obviously important in building and logging. Yet in every occupation there's a plumb line that determines whether our affairs are upright before God. By comparing our designs and ideas to a standard of right and wrong, we know how to build our businesses in favor with God and man. This universal plumb line is as simple and accurate as the rock and string. It's the Bible.

"All scripture is given by inspiration of God, and is profitable for doctrine, for reproof, for correction, for instruction in righteousness: That the man of God may be perfect, thoroughly furnished unto all good works" (2 Timothy 3:16,17).

Some folks mistakenly think that the Bible is for the religious world and not the business world. That kind of thinking leads any society into chaos. God intended His Word to be the standard measurement for industry and commerce. By it, men exchange goods and services in a way where everyone profits. Wherever men align their businesses with a practical understanding of the Bible, their society prospers.

Suppose you go to a garage sale and see a $600 table saw with a $200 sign on it. You've been looking for one just like it. Do you slap down the cash and buy it before someone else sees it? Maybe, but maybe not. As you talk with the woman holding the garage sale, you find that her husband died six months before and she is selling his tools to help make ends meet. She has no clue to the worth of the saw. What is the right thing to do?

Here's a quote from God's plumb line, "Woe unto them that decree unrighteous decrees…To turn aside the needy from judgment, and to take away the right from the poor of my people, that widows may be their prey, and that they may rob the fatherless!" (Isaiah 10:1,2).

If you ever take advantage of a widow in a business transaction, watch out. God will surely reprove you. Look through the Bible, observe God's heart for widows, and align with Him.

If you need that table saw, buy it. However, don't pay the $200 dollars she ignorantly asked for. If you have it, pay the $600 it's worth before someone else comes along and takes advantage of her. If you don't have $600, tell her what it's worth and offer her as much as you can. That's God's standard.

When I build a house and get up near the roof, it's my responsibility to provide safety rails and fall protection. The reason I know I'm responsible is because God's plumb line says so. "When thou buildest a new house, then thou shalt make a battlement for thy roof, that thou bring not blood upon thine house, if any man fall from thence" (Deuteronomy 22:8). If I don't care enough about the people that work around my house to provide protection for them, I don't align with God's care for people.

The Bible is full of practical instructions to teach us how to run businesses just like a plumb line tells Gary and Willie if a tree is straight. It is the standard for the world of commerce.

Some folks hire consultants to teach them lessons about running businesses and gathering money. Whether those lessons are true or not depend on how they look when held up beside the Bible. If these teachings are even slightly leaning from God's standard, they will lead into trouble.

The simple rock and string set the standard for every building in the world, from the skyscrapers of New York to the wooden huts in the Congo. The simple Bible, in the same way, sets the standard for business and work, from the most complex corporation to the lemonade stand on the sidewalk.

As you go about life's business, may you learn to be good builder, aligning all your affairs with God's Plumb Line.

Thus he showed me: and, behold, the Lord stood
upon a wall made by a plumbline,
with a plumbline in his hand. And the Lord said
unto me, Amos, what seest thou?

*And I said, A plumbline. Then said the Lord, Behold,
I will set a plumbline in the midst of my people
Israel...* (Amos 7:7,8)

Questions

• What does plumb mean?

• How can you make a tool that will display what's plumb?

• Why is it hard to tell which way a tree leans in the woods just by looking at it?

• What is God's plumb line for business decisions?

• Why should we align our business lives with this plumb line?

Promptly After, But Not Before

*A fool may make money, but it needs
a wise man to spend it.*

—C.H. Spurgeon

Never pay a man for his labor before he does the work."
"Never receive pay before you accomplish a task."

This is sound business advice to help you avoid painful experiences. If you don't believe me, just try it a time or two and you'll be convinced.

My father-in-law wanted a new seat for his motor home. He paid the full price when he ordered it. Somehow, the company couldn't get their hands on that seat. After five months and numerous requests, he sent his lawyer after them. Amazingly, the company quickly called to say that his seat was ready for installation as soon as they received the lawyer's letter.

I remember needing a part for my wood stove. The storeowner said I must pay full price before he could order it. Against my better judgment, I paid him. I was about to learn my lesson well. The part never came. He did give my money back a month later, after I contacted the Better Business Bureau and the state attorney general.

Just this week, I talked with the owner of the kitchen I'm currently remodeling. He was upset. His wife had gone to a countertop supplier and ordered a granite slab for their kitchen. They asked her to pay for the material and labor to install it before processing the order. She gave them their request. When he heard about it, he felt sick. He didn't blame his wife, because she didn't know. However, he's been in business long enough to imagine the trouble he might face in the near future.

No respectable company asks for the price of their labor ahead of time. It's understandable for a small business to request the cost of materials before installing them. And sometimes it's appropriate to ask for half the total bill beforehand to protect the contractor from questionable customers. Though it may be appropriate to pay something before work begins, never pay for labor before the workers finish the job.

What about when doing business with friends or with your family, should you pay for labor before they work? NO, DO NOT DO IT! Maybe you'll find an exception. There may be a time somewhere when you can get away with it. However, when you pay in advance, often before the deal is over somebody is disappointed.

Why am I so sure about this? Why is it worth writing a chapter about it? When you're in any business, you want to understand the nature of men and the nature of God. Business is not an activity where you try to get and keep all the money you can, though some foolish people work that way. For the Christian, business is the exchange of goods and services to meet needs and to display godliness.

A Christian man in business should conduct his affairs according to the character of God. His customers, suppliers, and associates should see God in the man as he transfers property and services from one person to another.

If you paid God for two pounds of roofing nails, how many pounds of nails would He give you in return? Would He put less than two pounds in your sack? Of course not! He may give you two pounds and a little more, but never any less. Why? Because He has enough and is generous with what He has.

You may not be able to give an extra eighth of a pound of nails with every sale, but you could give an extra nail or two. It may seem like a small amount, yet it's extra, and therefore it's generous. You'd rather give one nail too many than one nail too few. Why? Because that's the way God is.

God doesn't pay men before they work. It's after plowing, planting, and cultivating that the harvest comes. Jesus gave a parable about the workers in the vineyard and the generous householder. The householder agreed on a wage with the workers and paid them at the *end* of the day. "So when even was come, the lord of the vineyard saith unto his steward, Call the labourers, and give them their hire, beginning from the last unto the first" (Matthew 20:8).

Though God doesn't pay for work up front, He is very prompt to pay when it's completed and requires us to do so. "Thou shalt not oppress an hired servant that is poor and needy...At his day thou shalt give him his hire, neither shall the sun go down upon it; for he is poor, and setteth his heart upon it: lest he cry against thee unto the LORD, and it be sin unto thee" (Deuteronomy 24:14,15).

God does not pay for labor before completion because He understands the nature of man. If you feed a man without having him work first, he won't learn to work. The apostle Paul understood this principle and wrote, "For even when we were with you, this we commanded you, that if any would not work, neither should he eat" (2 Thessalonians 3:10). Full men do not work like hungry men.

God warned Israel, "...when thou shalt have eaten and be full; Then beware lest thou forget the LORD (Deuteronomy 6:11,12). When men are satisfied, they don't seek God the same as when they are longing. The needy seek Jesus, not the full.

Therefore, when you pay a man or a company before they work, they lose the motivation to complete their task. Why should they go out in the cold to work when they already have the money? They can wait for a better day. On the other hand, the man who needs the money will overcome many difficulties to finish the job because his eye is on the wealth he hopes to gain.

You might say, "Well, they should work just as hard because they have already been paid." You're right, they should. However, it's the nature of man to rest after receiving his reward.

I don't accept money for my labor before doing a job. As all men, I work best when hungry and looking ahead for payment. If someone pays me at the start of a job, it takes away my incentive. It makes me feel like I'm in debt. Instead of working simply because I want to, when prepaid, I work because I have to, to pay the obligation.

I hope you understand why you don't pay for labor before a man gives it, and why you don't accept pay before you earn it. It's a safeguard to your business. What's more, you're aligning your affairs with the character of God. He knows how to live, and it's worth your while to follow His design, especially in business.

May you always have a reputation for paying promptly and generously but not before the job is finished, because that's how God does it.

> *And, behold, I come quickly; and my reward is with me, to give every man according as his work shall be.* (Revelation 22:12)

Questions

- Who tends to work better, a full man or a hungry man?

- Why should you not pay a man for his labor before he works?

- Why should you not ask for money before you work?

- Why pay promptly, generously, and after the work is completed?

Sidestepping Discouragement

We could never learn to be brave and patient,
if there were only joy in the world.

—Helen Keller

Discouragement defeats a worker. It grows from roots of laziness, lack of vision, and selfishness. Discouraged people think too much about themselves and too little about God. With that said, I must confess, I have frequently faced discouragement. Within me is the desire for courage. I want to live with a clear mind, holding my head up, fearlessly defeating all my enemies with no thoughts except victory. That has not always been the case for me.

At age eighteen, I lived alone in an apartment above the Springfield Cleaners, worked for Hennen Trenching installing underground utilities, and attended a local university. The events of that season of my life revealed that I possessed a frail mind, which easily tumbled into discouragement.

Often I questioned and accused myself,

"What are you doing?"

"Where are you going in life?"

"You are wasting your productive years."

"You'll end in failure."

When I thought too much about the future, clouds of discouragement rolled in. Occasionally the storms were so dark that I felt I had gone crazy.

The feelings lasted for days and even weeks at a time. During those periods, I sat for hours staring at the wall, neglecting school assignments, my laundry, relationships, and worst of all, my God. When the clouds lifted and life looked good again, my neglected responsibilities overwhelmed me and brought back the discouragement. What a vicious circle!

One day, it dawned on me. When discouraged, I get behind; when behind, I get discouraged. Why not keep up with my responsibilities whether I feel like it or not. Then, when my discouragement is over, my work will be too! I tried it and it worked!

A discouraged man doesn't have to stop living. He doesn't have to wait until he feels joyful to accomplish his work. When you are committed to a job that you don't feel like doing, do it anyway. Waiting until you feel like working promotes laziness, destroys your productivity, and clouds your mind. By the time you feel like working again your tasks have multiplied.

Keeping up on tasks is particularly important if you are, or plan to be, self-employed. The company whistle, the eye of a superintendent, the fear of losing your job may motivate you to work for your employer. However, when *you* are the boss, you need a mind that rules your body.

Dale Kast contracted to build a house in the small coastal town of Yachats (pronounced *Yah-hots*). He hired me to install the interior woodwork. High on a hill overlooking the Pacific Ocean, I worked alone nailing trim around windows that opened to beautiful views of ocean waves, spouting whales, and colorful sunsets. Dale continually complained of the local workers. On sunny days, it was too nice to work; they'd all go fishing. On rainy days, they didn't show up; it was too wet to work.

A man runs a poor business who only works when he feels like it. Production doesn't wait for your feelings. Go to work. Do a good job of it and your emotions usually follow. However, if they don't and you still don't feel like working at the end of the day, at least your project is complete. Which is better, to feel lazy at the end of a day with the job finished, or to feel lazy with the job still in front of you? Discouragement is allowing your mind to keep your body from doing what it ought to do.

The leaves in the yard need raking. It's your job. Your afternoon is free but it's raining lightly. Everybody knows that human bodies don't melt when exposed to water. Still, some thought of discouragement sneaks into your mind to announce, "It's too wet to work outside." Once allowed into your mind and permitted to stay, that one discouraging thought opens the door to his buddies who enter declaring, "By all means work any other day but not today!"

Is your body able to do the job? Yes. Forget the phantoms in your mind and let your body at it! Get a coat. Slap on your hat. Walk straight for the rake and begin. Soon you'll be finished!

Keep discouraging intruders out of your mind, and your body will complete your responsibilities and fulfill your God-given dreams. Should any discouraging thought get past the front door and into the hallway of your mind, sidestep him. Go around and accomplish the task in spite of him. Don't even waste the time to put up a fight. In less time than it takes to destroy the intruder, you might finish the project. Often finishing a project is just the thing to overcome discouragement.

The procrastinator's mind fills with cloudy thoughts: rake the leaves on the next free afternoon, write that thank-you note soon, clean up my room sometime, visit Mr. Booher about a job when I'm free. Thoughts of disagreeable projects run round and round in his head, getting heavier with each lap. He spends more time thinking about what he doesn't want to do than the time it takes to do it. The result is mental instability.

How do you clear up this mental rat race? Ignore your excuses. Ignore your emotions. Pick a disagreeable task on your "to do" list and begin to work. When finished, take another one. One by one, eliminate them. Meanwhile, when new responsibilities arrive, jump at the opportunity to work. Do it! The result is a clear mind, free to imagine roads of adventure and the heart to walk down them.

God has not given us the spirit of fear to back down from work. He has given us the spirit of power and a sound mind to do the tasks before us. A good worker keeps a clear mind by tackling his work, especially when he doesn't feel like it.

> *So built we the wall; and all the wall was joined*
> *together unto the half thereof:*
> *for the people had a mind to work.*
> (Nehemiah 4:6)

Questions

- What is discouragement?

- The workers in Yachats accomplished little. Why?

- Describe one way to get out of discouragement.

- What is the difference between a discouraged mind and a sound mind?

Keeping Your Word

God did not call me to be successful.
God called me to be faithful.

—Mother Teresa

I like getting older. Every day, my experience proves the Bible is true. I've seen God fulfill His promises. I've watched the righteous finish life with honor. I've observed the wicked end in confusion. I know how the world was created and can see through some of the foolish theories that seem wise for a season. Personal relationships prosper or divide based on their alignment to principles found in the pages of Scripture. I haven't seen everything; nevertheless, by reading the Bible every day and by watching life, I've come to this practical conclusion: the Bible accurately describes reality.

Here is a biblical truth that proves itself real when applied to the construction world: "LORD, who shall abide in thy tabernacle? who shall dwell in thy holy hill?...He that sweareth to his own hurt, and changeth not" (Psalm 15:1,4).

I was scheduled to frame a house for a man in Eugene. He postponed the starting date many times. An older lady wanted me to install a doggie door for her little bug-eyed, flat-nosed dog. "I'll do it next Monday," I said. Later, the man from Eugene called to say he wanted his job started on Monday also.

What would you do? The doggie door was half a day's work and I usually didn't charge her a full rate. The framing job would give me more than a month's wages. Should I put off the lady or the man? I had given my word—was I strong enough to keep it even to my hurt?

I reasoned, "Happy is the guy who makes a commitment and sticks to it." Then I told the man, "I'll start Tuesday." Angrily he said, "Either start Monday or forget the job."

I wanted that job. Nevertheless, I said, "I have a more important job Monday. I'll gladly come Tuesday."

"Don't bother," he replied, "I'll get somebody else."

I didn't feel happy about losing that job until six months later when I talked with the plumber. "Hey, I thought you were going to frame that house in Eugene," he said. "What happened?"

"I had too much work," I replied.

"That job became a nightmare for everyone," he continued. "It was good you got out of it."

A Bible verse, applied to a doggie door, gave me stable guidelines for making a decision that saved me a lot of trouble.

Situations aren't always so clear, neither are they painless. Still, we must trust that God's ways are true and fulfill our part of the bargain, even when it hurts.

When my friend Jon says he's coming at eight to install a sink, he arrives at eight. He doesn't show up ten minutes late with some excuse. He arranges his morning and attempts only what he has time to do. I've even adjusted my watch as I saw Jon drive up—he's that accurate. I like the stability he brings to the job site by his determination to keep his word.

I don't understand all that happened when Jesus was in the garden of Gethsemane. He had purposed to do His Father's will. He knew death awaited Him in Jerusalem, yet it appears He began to realize it would hurt more than He imagined. Jesus didn't alter His course because of the coming pain. He did what He said He would and died. The result is a life forever with the Father, abiding in His holy hill. And not for Jesus alone, but for all who believe in Him.

"Tasha, I'll be over at five tonight to help you wash your dog," Jensen said as they left the park.

At four, Gabe calls to ask Jensen if he can come to Camp Putt for a game of miniature golf.

What should Jensen do? He should thank Gabe for thinking about him, and decline the offer. He might enjoy playing golf more than washing a dog, but the man who swears to his own hurt and

changes not is better off than the man who only does what he wants, when he wants to.

It's easier to keep words in your mouth than to try to fulfill them after you speak. Knowing that I must do what I say motivates me to say as little as possible. Before committing to a job, or other responsibilities, I had better stop for a moment, consider the options, and count the cost. I've saved myself, and others, a lot of grief by simply saying, "No," when I can't.

Why is keeping your word such a big deal? First, it's because God keeps His. If you say you want to follow God, follow Him. Second, keeping your word is a sure way to bring stability to your family, friends, and community. They can count on you.

Other men may not keep their word. That's no reason why you shouldn't. God doesn't play by their rules, and He's the One who controls the universe. He can take care of them. You keep your word.

Since you promised to follow God, there are times when you shouldn't keep your promise to men. Suppose someday you promise to marry a girl, and then you learn that she is already married. Do you keep your promise? Of course not! You are not under an obligation to do what's wrong. Or, maybe you say you'll buy a car tomorrow. That night you learn it's a stolen car. Do you buy it as you said you would? No!

If you discover that what you promised to do is wrong, lose money or pay whatever it costs, but don't do it.

There are times when you should not keep your word. If you promised to show up on a job tomorrow and you wake up with a highly contagious disease, the kind thing to do would be to call up those expecting you and explain the situation. They'd appreciate your change of plans more than having your presence and getting your sickness. The Bible gives us stable guidelines for how to live in love. Keeping your word, or making *acceptable* arrangements to do otherwise, is living in love.

Is there any recovery when you fail to keep your word? Of course! There is always a path for the man who falls short.

I remember promising to meet a realtor at a house that needed repairs. I completely forgot about it! It wasn't until the next day that I remembered the appointment. I felt sick. Surely she must have stood around for an hour or so waiting for me to show up. There was only one course of action for me. Going to the nearest florist, I bought an expensive arrangement of flowers and drove to her office. Along with the flowers, I offered an apology for missing the meeting. She accepted my confession and said that I didn't need to buy flowers. However, I wanted it to cost me something so that I'd remember to keep my word in the future.

God sets up challenges for the man who purposes to keep his word. Promises will become almost impossible to fulfill. You'll find yourself forced to give up things you've wanted for what you committed to. There'll be struggles, victories, and maybe some defeats. At the finish of the course, you'll boldly proclaim to any who will hear, "God's word is true. The man who swears to his own hurt and changes not, will find stability and experience the joy of God's presence."

Therefore whosoever heareth these sayings of mine, and doeth them, I will liken him unto a wise man, which built his house upon a rock: And the rain descended, and the floods came, and the winds blew, and beat upon that house; and it fell not: for it was founded upon a rock.
(Matthew 7:24,25)

Questions

- Why is keeping your word such a big deal?

- If Jensen had gone golfing, what would Tasha think of him?

- The next time Jensen said that he would help Tasha, would Tasha trust him?

- When should you *not* keep your word?

- What should you do when you've failed to do what you promised?

The Donut Race

No man who is in a hurry is quite civilized.

—Will Durant

The boys didn't plan to race. A cat doesn't plan to chase a mouse. Any healthy cat that sees a running mouse chases it without a thought. A mouse seeing a chasing cat must run. It's instinct in a cat, in a mouse, and sometimes in boys.

Before school one morning, Rob and Butch decided to meet about five miles away from their homes, at the Dunkin' Donuts shop.

"See you there," shouted Butch as he zipped out of the parking lot in his 1969 Volkswagen convertible. Rob ran to his 1965 Chevy Malibu, jerked open the door, and jumped in. The mouse had run down the street and the cat had to chase.

Butch wasn't the perfect driver. However, this morning he decided to drive the speed limit no matter what the cat behind him did. He wasn't going to give in to his strong urge to race. He resigned himself to enjoy the drive, calmly. He drove at the 35 mph speed limit with one eye on the road and the other on his rear-view mirror looking for his friend.

Here came the cat. Rob sailed by doing close to 50 mph, wearing the victor's grin as he took the lead.

There were three stoplights between home and Dunkin' Donuts. The first one turned red ahead of Rob. Regretfully he came to a stop and anxiously looked in his rear-view mirror at the steadily approaching Volkswagen.

Butch casually putted along like a Sunday driver. Rob chomped at the bit.

Butch, knowing the light was changing, held his speed steady. Just before entering the intersection, the light turned green and he went through, passing the Chevy at a standstill. As Butch passed, Rob stomped on the gas and squealed off the line.

The next light was a short block away and the Volkswagen slipped under it just before it turned red. Rob, who was slightly behind, had to stop. He howled as he sat motionless watching Butch drive away.

Butch casually pulled into the parking lot and walked in the door. He perched on a stool at the coffee bar and lazily looked over his shoulder when the dejected Rob walked in.

"Where have you been, Rob?" asked Butch. "I've been waiting all morning for you."

As Rob climbed on the stool beside Butch, he lamented, "I would have won if that light hadn't changed."

Without any sympathy and with a nose a little higher than proper, Butch added, "Who was racing?"

I tell you this true story because it illustrates the difference between haste and speed. Today's society values speed as a chief virtue, but it often mistakes speed for haste.

God's not impressed with hastiness. He says in Proverbs, "The thoughts of the diligent tend only to plenteousness; but of every one that is hasty only to want" (21:5). And, "Seest thou a man that is hasty in his words? There is more hope of a fool than of him" (29:20). And once more, "He that hasteth with his feet sinneth" (19:2).

We live in a fast-paced world. If you don't want to lose what you have, if you don't want to be a fool, and if you don't want to live in sin, it's important to learn the distinction between haste and speed.

You'll know when you are being hasty if you stop for a moment and check yourself with a few questions: Do you sense a tension in your stomach? Are you trying to accomplish more than time allows? Are you in such a hurry that you are making foolish mistakes? Do you feel like Rob, squealing your tires and then braking for red lights? If these are your experiences, you can be sure that your actions will not lead to abundance. Instead, you'll make foolish decisions and miss a peaceful walk with God.

Hasty people miss God because God is never in a hurry. He doesn't change His pace to walk with people. He requires people to change their pace to walk with Him. A man rushing through life, running over everything and anyone that gets in his way, will not hear the voice of God. His hurried efforts create too much chaos for him to enjoy God's presence.

It's not that speed is bad. It's just that good speed is never hasty.

Light travels at 186,000 miles a second, yet it's never in a hurry. You don't see it scurrying, slamming into walls, or stumbling over stuff. It's not frustrated, worried, or irritated. Light obediently travels the speed God created it to travel, calmly, quietly, and fast.

On the job yesterday I faced the challenge of speed versus haste. I worked alone in a new house, installing the surrounds and casings on the second-floor windows. To finish them all in one day I had to be quick.

I rapidly set up my sliding compound saw, plugged in the compressor, and strung out my hoses and air guns. With clipboard in hand, I hustled to measure each window. Back at the saw, the cutting began.

That old hasty feeling started creeping into my stomach. I rushed to get the next board with a sense of urgency. Oops. That board was too short. I cut 34 and 11/16ths instead of 34 and 13/16ths. That wasn't my only mistake. I got confused about what sill went where and how to get the most out of the lengths of available boards. Frustration began tightening up the muscles in my shoulders. My joyful whistling stopped.

There are two reasons why I can't afford to be hasty. One is that homeowners and builders expect high-quality work. I need to produce tight mitered joints, straight sills, and consistent reveals between the casing and surrounds. Hasty work is never very good. The second reason is that hastiness prevents me from joyfully walking with God each moment of the day.

Therefore, when that hasty spirit began to rise, I knew I needed to slow down. My desire to impress the builder with how much I could accomplish in a day caused my hastiness. Confessing that fault, I resigned myself to simply work well and accomplish what I could.

A hymn returned to my heart and a whistle to my lips. I concentrated on each measurement and cut carefully. My movements became smooth instead of choppy. My speed picked up but without that element of haste. The mistakes stopped. I still climbed the stairs two steps at a time and walked briskly; however, my heart was at rest.

At quitting time I had reached my goal. All the windows were finished and no joints needed excuses. The best part was experiencing the joy of God's presence throughout the day. I finished refreshed and with a happy heart.

Don't think that I always throw haste out of my life at the first sign of him. It's because I've spent so many days foolishly following his advice that the days without haste seem so sweet. I desire to live life without a hasty heart. I think you would too. It's how God intends us to live.

I'm not encouraging you to be a slow worker. There are times you need to be quick about your business. Maybe you have heard your parents or your boss say that you need to speed up. If so, then it's probably true.

Many practical things will increase your production without being hasty. Don't talk any more than you have to. Concentrate on your work. Don't let yourself get sidetracked thinking about other things. Finish your current job before considering the next project. Start early. Enjoy your breaks but get back to work promptly. Go to bed at night. Eat well.

If you are serious about being a fast worker, you'll not only do these things but you'll ask God to show you other areas where you might be wasting time. He'll give you ideas, if you're willing to obey them. You can be a speedy worker and maintain a restful heart at the same time.

The ability to work quickly and skillfully, and with an awareness of God's presence, is a great privilege. Don't let hastiness rob you of this simple joy.

"Hey Rob, do you want to race to school?" hollered Butch as he left the donut shop.

"No thanks," answered Rob. "I'll just putt along and meet you there."

An inheritance may be gotten hastily at the beginning; but the end thereof shall not be blessed. (Proverbs 20:21)

Questions

- Why did Rob speed on his way to the donut shop?

- What is the difference between haste and speed?

- If you were paid by the hour, why would your boss want you to work faster?

- What is the greatest thing you lose by being hasty?

The Making of a President

The nature of our government demanded a quality
of individual responsibility and a capacity for
self-government never before required...

—Noah Webster

Every man is responsible for ruling over something. If nothing else, a man is required to rule his own heart. God ordained men to have dominion over the animals, to rule well as husbands and fathers. God often assigns men to lead on job sites, in small groups, in the church, in government positions, and even in world arenas. Where does a boy learn to be an effective ruler? The following imaginary story offers one explanation.

"Hey Josh, why are you so gloomy?" asked Trevor.

"I've just come from my Government class. We're studying the United States presidential cabinet. It's boring. Why should I learn that stuff? I'll never be president and I'd rather play basketball," replied Josh.

"That's exactly how I felt," said Trevor, "until the day Dad heard me complaining. He gave me the motivation not only to study about the cabinet, but also to make it a part of my life. I may never hold the presidency of the United States, but I began that day to prepare for it."

"What did he say to change your mind?"

"It wasn't just his words. It was his strong emotions that affected me. After my complaint, he looked serious. He asked me to sit on the couch. Looking me straight in the eye, he said that the usefulness of my life depended on me learning to rule over my own spirit, my own soul, and my own heart.

"Normally, Dad doesn't talk like that. I had obviously pushed one of his buttons. He said that if I diligently ruled over the daily business of my life, I would be like a walled city or a secure country.

"He wanted me to think of my life as a personal nation. He asked me if I would lead my personal country with liberty and justice, or if I'd be an example of Proverbs 25:28, 'He that hath no rule over his own spirit is like a city that is broken down, and without walls?' "

"What did you tell him?" asked Josh.

"I told him that I didn't know how to run my life like a country. Then I asked him if he had any ideas about what I could do."

"What did he say?"

"Dad said that's precisely the reason for studying about the executive department and the president's cabinet. Understanding the responsibilities of each cabinet member and personally applying those responsibilities is an excellent way for a man to learn to run his own life or personal nation."

"Wow," said Josh, "I've never thought of that. I didn't realize that studying government had anything to do with me."

"I didn't either, but it made sense when Dad put it like that. He said that I might never be the president of our country, but I was the president of my heart. Someday I might be the president of a home. And who knows, I just might be asked to be the president of the United States when I grow up. If that's the case, I'd better start getting ready now, because it's a big job. If I rule my life like a president today, I'll be more qualified for the position forty years from now."

"You're getting a little too lofty for me. We're just kids," interrupted Josh.

"I might be a kid, but I'm going to follow my dad's advice and start thinking like a man. Someday I'll be one. And I'll be one a lot sooner if I start thinking like one today. I'm not going to think like just any ol' man either. I'm going to think like a president."

"That sounds strange," said Josh.

"Dad says we live in a day when good men are called strange, and strange men are called good. I'm going to be a good man even if it means being called strange…I didn't think you'd call me that!" snapped Trevor.

"Easy does it. I'm just not used to thinking like this. It's new to me. I like the idea but it's…different."

"Sorry, I guess I was a little sensitive," apologized Trevor. "Do you think you'd want to try thinking like the president with me?"

"Well, I can try. But, like I said, it's new to me. Where do we start?" asked Josh.

"Dad says to start by thoroughly learning about the executive department and how it functions. Then we'll try to run our lives by the principles we observe there."

"How is a teenager supposed to live like a presidential cabinet member?" asked Josh.

"Dad quoted to me what somebody named Thomas Carlyle once said: 'Our main business is not to see what lies dimly at a distance, but to do what lies clearly at hand.' Then he began to list the different departments. He told me what they did in Washington D.C., and gave me suggestions how I could order my life here, just like the committees were designed to function there."

"Give me an example," asked Josh.

"One member of the president's cabinet is the secretary of state. He oversees foreign affairs. All relationships with other countries fall under his jurisdiction. His duties include correspondence, planning treaties, visitations, and interacting with foreign embassies. Any nation wanting official communications with the United States approaches through the State Department. There's the pattern. The question is, how do we use this pattern to think like a man?

"Dad said if I consider myself as a nation, and other people I know as other nations, all the secretary of state's duties are guidelines for me. Has anyone tried to correspond with me by letter or phone? I need to contact them quickly just as the State Department would respond to a foreign country. Do I have problems in any relationships that need attention? Should I plan any visits, or invite others to be my guests?"

"That reminds me," interrupted Josh. "I told Zack I would come over and see him. He's been sick and I forgot all about it!"

"You catch on fast! That's exactly what Dad wanted me to learn. Thinking about the secretary of state reminded you of a responsibility you need to fulfill. If you do it the next chance you get, you're ruling your nation wisely."

"That was easy. What are some of the other departments?" asked Josh.

"Well, one of my favorites is the Department of Transportation. The secretary of transportation is responsible for safe and efficient travel for trucks, trains, airplanes, and ships. His job is to make sure that goods and people may travel freely, anywhere in the nation."

Before Trevor could explain how to apply it, Josh shouted. "I know how that works! My Department of Transportation takes care of my bike. I need to oil my chain. It squeaks so bad that I can't sneak by the dog on Third Street anymore. He's waiting to chase me while I'm still a block away. A good secretary of transportation would have taken care of that before now. Boy, I can see that my personal country is in bad shape and you've only told me about two of the departments. How many are there?"

"I think there are about thirteen or so," answered Trevor, "They change from time to time, depending on the needs of the country."

"Wow, that's a lot," exclaimed Josh. "Can you tell me another one?"

"I'd like to, but I just heard Mom calling me for dinner. I think that government book under your arm has the list in it. Stop by tomorrow after class and maybe we can come up with more ideas."

"I will," said Josh as he left for home.

At the dinner table, Trevor told his father about the conversation. "Hey Dad, I told Josh about the lesson you taught me on personal government."

"You mean about making comparisons between the executive department and our own lives?" returned Dad.

"Yes. He couldn't understand what I meant at first. Then once he caught onto the idea, he got excited. I only wish I knew more about what each department does. The more I understand, the easier it is to make analogies, and the more it applies to my life. Could we look at the responsibilities of cabinet members after dinner? I'd like to be ready for Josh when he comes over tomorrow."

"Sure, I'd be glad to help you. It makes me happy that you're interested in gaining wisdom, especially when you apply it to your life."

"Thanks, Dad. When I consider thinking like the president, it makes me want to make wise decisions throughout the day, instead of just doing whatever comes to mind. It's a change for me, and I like it."

"Trevor, most young folks who study the United States government see it as musty old facts. That's not the case for you. I hope these truths will live in your heart, enough to change the way you keep your room, the way you treat your home, your community, and your nation.

"You look like you have a question, Son," said Dad.
"I do," smiled Trevor. "May I have more mashed potatoes?"

> **For if a man know not how to rule his own house,**
> **how shall he take care of the church of God?**
> (1 Timothy 3:5)

Questions

• Why did Josh find the U.S. Government class boring?

• What changed Trevor's mind about the class?

• Why was Trevor's dad pleased with him?

• Pick a department of the president's cabinet from the following list. Can you see how the responsibilities of that department might apply to your personal nation? (The more you understand the responsibilities of each department the easier it will be to ask questions.)

Executive Departments:
State
Treasury
Defense
Justice
Interior
Agriculture
Commerce
Labor
Health and Human Services
Housing and Urban Development
Transportation
Energy
Education
Homeland Security

The Morning Song

The Lord taught me that the first business I needed to attend to every day was to have my spirit happy in the Lord. My first concern shouldn't be thinking of ways to serve and glorify the Lord, but rather, how to get my spirit into a happy state, and how to nourish my inner man.

—George Mueller

My favorite time of the day is just before dawn. Most of the night creatures are making their way to bed. Most of the day creatures are still asleep. Frequently, the wind dies down. The anticipation of the coming day seems to hush the forest.

In the summer, the voice of a happy bird breaks this stillness. He chirps a note or two as he tunes up. Then he quietly sings his God-given song. As his volume increases, another bird joins in, and then another, until the whole crowd of early risers belts out a morning concert.

Though I've identified fifty-six different types of birds on our property, the main morning singers are the rufous-sided towhees, fox sparrows, song sparrows, black-headed grosbeaks, winter wrens, and robins. Each bird sings his song regardless of what the others sing. They blend to make one choir, singing for the pleasure of their Maker.

The robins clearly dominate the choir. Perched on fence posts or apple trees, they lift their beaks and give it their all. They remind me of scenes I used to see as a kid. A car would drive through town with a sign on its back declaring a destination and their determination to get there. "Alaska or Bust" was one of those signs. If robins wore bumper stickers, and you can imagine why they don't, they just might have one that says, "Sing or Bust."

In a little while, they'll all go about their business of gathering worms for their babies, chasing moths, and fighting predators away from their nests. However, first thing in the morning there's nothing more natural than to sing until the sun appears.

At sunset, the birds gather again on favorite limbs and fence tops for a quieter version of the morning's praise. The evening song may consist of the same notes and melodies, but it's without eager anticipation. At dusk, the songs seem more restful. It's almost as if the birds are giving thanks. They sing until one by one, they head off to their beds.

Creation expresses the nature of God. If we had the ears to hear and the eyes to see, every plant, animal, and rock would teach us God's attributes. They'd explain the paths of life and show us how to walk them. "But ask now the beasts, and they shall teach thee; and the fowls of the air, and they shall tell thee: Or speak to the earth, and it shall teach thee: and the fishes of the sea shall declare unto thee" (Job 12:7,8).

What can a young man learn about life and work by listening to birds before the sun rises and when it sets? If he's attentive, he'll learn to start each day with a joyful song, and end with thanksgiving.

Most of us have all the food we need to survive, as close as our refrigerators. We usually live without fear of predators. Yet, do we groan as we think of getting out of bed? Do we complain about the work ahead of us? Or are we like the birds, whose hearts are so joyful that they must sing lest they burst? Life for a bird in the summer is a dawn-to-dark fight for the survival of the next generation. Yet they sing every morning and every night.

Joy is God's gift to the man who will receive it. God provides everything you'll need today and protects you from every evil. He completely controls the whole world and considers every step you take. Besides all this, He wants to communicate with you. Shouldn't that be enough to give you a measure of confidence and delight?

God's presence and joy are everywhere in the world except in the hearts of people who refuse Him. Those who resist God find His presence troublesome. For some, even the thought of God is enough to make them angry. He doesn't force Himself on these

folks. He gives them the freedom to accept or reject Him. Even the Christian who has cried to Jesus for salvation may choose to push God away in daily experience.

If you have walked with God very long, there may have been times when you've pushed Him away by your complaining and ungrateful attitude. You've felt Him leave your side just as a dove would fly out an open window. The sick feeling you sense when you've done wrong and won't repent warns that you are shoving God out of your life; and with Him goes the joy of your heart.

Every man has a choice. When the birds start singing in the morning, some men awake with a WA-HOO! and jump into the day's adventures. Others would like to get a hand on those birds and wring their little necks.

It's your privilege as a Christian to begin each day assured of God's presence and provision and convinced there is nothing coming that's too hard for Him. You may be sure that God has kept His eye on you from before your birth and will do so through eternity. Today you may not feel well; maybe you didn't get much sleep last night. Your body and mind might sense the struggles of this world. That's no reason to let your spirit give up.

It's your choice whether you'll keep God's words in your mind or not. Even when your body is sore, worn out, or broken, you can still decide to wake up with a measure of cheerfulness. A merry heart does good like a medicine. If you refuse a merry heart, your broken spirit will dry up your bones.

When you choose to sing, sing your God-given song. A winter wren who thought he should sing like a song sparrow would start every day frustrated at his failure to do what he couldn't. One man might begin the day by expressing his joy with a beautiful melody on his piano. Another might communicate his appreciation by quietly humming a tune he learned as a child.

The first line of my favorite morning song is, "Holy, Holy, Holy, Lord God Almighty, early in the morning my song shall rise to Thee…" However, I rarely sing it aloud as I awaken. Often I'm out of bed some time before the rest of my family. Robust songs at that time may be pleasant to me, but not to those sound asleep. Therefore, I quietly hum until I get into the woodshop or the garden house where I can express joy without being a curse to the others.

Some days I don't feel like singing. Those are the days I need it most. When I awake with a start at 4:30 and remember that concrete trucks will show up at six and I still have a half hour's work to do, it's easy to let fears creep in. Thoughts like these try to scare me: "You won't be ready in time. The trucks will be waiting at eighty dollars an hour and you can't make it." My way of escape is to purpose to sing a morning song. As I sing, God reminds me that He is in control and nothing is too hard for Him.

I hope that you have grown up a cheerful boy, rejoicing in God's presence each morning, singing joyfully as you get out of bed. I didn't. I grew up grumpy, not only in the mornings, but throughout much of the day. I didn't have a reason to sing, for I didn't know God. Just because I grew up a grouch, I don't have to remain one, and neither do you.

God has given you the freedom, if you'll receive it, to begin each day singing and making melody in your heart to the Lord, thanking Him for all things. You choose what you think about as you lie in bed after awakening. Do you think about unpleasant things? Do you let fears into your mind? Or do you let your heart express its joy and trust in God through a simple song of praise?

The man who begins each day singing his song, like the robin on the fence, will tend to be a productive worker as he accepts life's challenges with a happy heart. Moreover, if he retains God in his mind while he works, when it's time to return to his bed at night, he'll still have a song in his heart, a song of thanks to his faithful Creator.

May you be that man.

But I will sing of thy power; yea, I will sing aloud of thy mercy in the morning: for thou hast been my defence and refuge in the day of my trouble.
(Psalm 59:16)

Questions

- When you wake up in the morning are you usually cheerful or grumpy?

- How do you choose which one you will be?

- Name a place where a man can keep God from entering.

- What do you get when you refuse to let God dwell in your mind?

- What is something you can do to wake up cheerful?

The Process

When a man chops his own
firewood it warms him twice.

Have you ever ridden in a car when the timing is off a few degrees? Ka-pow-pow-puh-pow. The whole car shakes, jolts, and sounds like a Fourth of July celebration. Few cars drive very far in that condition.

Though not like the car I just described, my pickup is showing signs of losing its timing. It's not starting well and when I turn off the key it wants to keep running. Climbing hills, it rattles and pings. I can change the sparkplugs, distributor cap and rotor, but that's about the limit of my mechanical ability. Those of you who successfully work on engines have my respect. I'm sure it's relatively simple, but I've never learned how.

Like engines, sometimes our hearts get out of time. They begin running poorly, leaving us frustrated, discouraged, and sometimes angry. Few of us like to admit we're running rough, even when folks around us clearly hear it. Though it may seem complicated, like repairing an engine seems to me, resetting the timing of our hearts is really quite simple.

The standard by which a man tunes his heart is the nature and attributes of God. When a heart aligns with Him, it runs smoothly no matter how rough the road. When a heart is out of tune with God, even on the best pavement, the ride is bumpy. Therefore, the way to tune your heart is to learn what God is like and let your heart follow Him.

God possesses limitless attributes. You'll never run out of discoveries of His nature; it's a lifelong adventure. With each attribute you see, and align with, you experience the feeling similar to driving a newly tuned car.

I'd like to describe one of God's attributes and the pleasure that comes with living in tune with Him.

My wife, Janet, and I stood looking at the dirt we leveled for a new lawn. "I'm glad we aren't buying sod," she said.

"Why is that?" I asked.

"Because I like to watch things grow."

We didn't purchase speedy sod because my wife likes to see seeds scattered on the dirt. She enjoys the anticipation, wondering what day the hint of green will appear. Last Thursday we saw that first hint. Now, every morning we look out the window to check the progress. Every day it changes. We have to smile; it looks so good. Janet knew this happiness was too much to miss by purchasing ready grown sod. She also saved a hundred and fifteen dollars.

We wanted to replace our old freezer. I thought we should go buy one. My wife gave kind resistance to my plans.

"I'm saving for it," she said.

"We've got the money, why don't we go buy it now?" I asked.

"I'd rather not, if it's okay, because I'm saving a little each month. In two months I'll have enough put aside to buy it."

Instead of rushing to buy whatever enters her mind, my wife likes saving for it. The process of watching her stash of money grow makes her happy.

Anticipation is sometimes more enjoyable than an actual event. My wife has discovered a secret for getting the maximum enjoyment from life, with the least expense: enjoy the process. Janet has learned from experience that *process* is an attribute of God. If you read the Bible or explore nature, you'll see it everywhere. God likes to do things in a process.

God Himself is the same yesterday, today, and forever. However, when He formed the universe, He created an arena of process. He could have made the world in one day. Instead, He took six. As He completed each part He paused and said within Himself, "This is good." On the seventh day He stopped, rested, and enjoyed it all. He could have made people mature at birth, but He didn't. He decided that people should take years to reach adulthood. We live in the middle of a huge process of growth and decay.

God reserves the right to intervene in these processes and work instant miracles when He wants. However, He usually limits His work on earth within a process of time.

God says that His kingdom is like a mustard seed that starts small and grows into a large plant. It's like a farmer who goes to sleep at night and in the morning finds his plants have grown more, yet he doesn't know how.

God sets the speed of life. We tend to run too fast or too slow, causing ourselves trouble and frustration. If we want a smooth running life, we must learn to appreciate and align with the process God uses.

Today's technology aims at one major goal: to obtain what we think, the moment we think it. How can we cook our food within moments of getting hungry? Buy a microwave oven. How can I talk with my friend the moment I think of him? Get a cell phone. It's no longer enough to have Internet access. We want high-speed Internet so the moment we desire a Web site, it flashes on the screen.

Many people get frustrated with God because He doesn't jump when they push a button. With a button the garage door rolls up, with a button the CD player starts, and with a push of a button, flames jump from the logs of a gas fireplace. When they pray to God and He doesn't respond within the second, they run somewhere else for an answer. Unless we understand that God works within a process, we'll run ahead in our own foolish ways before He has prepared a path and given us the wisdom to walk it.

In the Old Testament God revealed to Daniel an event that would surely happen though the time appointed was yet to come. Daniel lacked full knowledge of the matter and began fasting until he could understand more. Three weeks later an angel arrived with the wisdom he wanted. The angel said that he started coming the

day Daniel first set himself to fast, but it took twenty-one days to get past the prince of Persia.

Why did God let the prince of Persia delay the message to Daniel? Does that prince have any power to withstand God? Of course not! For some reason the delay was part of God's time schedule. His answer to Daniel came at the right moment in the process.

When we lose the ability to enjoy the process, we try to shorten the time between when we want something and when we get it. Our focus tends to be only on our desire and views anything that keeps us from it as a disagreeable obstacle.

God creates and enjoys the process of life; we tend to want the goal. Unless we change to align with Him, our lives become an exercise in frustration. On the other hand, if we do learn to appreciate the processes of life we'll find rest and joy in the middle of life instead of hoping for it at the end.

The opposite of going too fast is the problem of longing to go too slow. Process assumes a change. Many of us don't like change. Refusing to accept the changes will leave our hearts frustrated, discouraged, and out of step with life.

In the early 1970s we framed houses with clear fir lumber. That's not the case now. Today's two by fours have large knots and some even have bark on the corners! It won't do any good to complain. It's a change I must learn to live with.

My children are continually changing. If I treat them like three-year-olds, now that they are in their twenties, I have a problem.

My body is changing too. I can't lift what I could twenty years ago. It's time to learn some creativity instead of straining my back. It's part of life's process. By aligning with God's nature and process, I work slower and hopefully smarter now. If I refuse to live His speed, I'll end up in bed with a pinched nerve in my back. I have learned that lesson from experience.

I might like the old ways but that's not life for me any more. Unless I want to live as a bitter old complainer, I must choose to get in time with God and find my resting place enjoying the pace of His process. So do you.

Beware of trying to get things too fast and watch out for hanging onto things too long. Both errors will keep you from living in tune with God.

To every thing there is a season, and a time to every purpose under the heaven.

(Ecclesiastes 3:1)

Questions

- Why did Janet want to plant grass seed instead of laying an instant lawn?

- Why did God choose to create life as a process?

- What happens if we want to live faster than the speed of His process?

- What happens if we don't want to change when He does?

- Can you think of a time when you have wanted life to be faster or slower than God did?

- What happens when you willingly live according to the speed of God's processes?

Treasure in Our Box

The Pacific Northwest has about 25,000 species of bugs. This number is a guess, of course...I hope you realize that to a hard-core bugster like myself, every single one of those 25,000 species has the potential to be wonderfully interesting in its own right.

—John Acorn

What kind of beetle dresses like a basketball referee? I saw one last summer on a neighbor's shed. The creature's body, including his thick antennas, measured two and a half inches. His black and white striped uniform caught my attention.

Later, while thumbing through my *Bugs of Washington and Oregon* field guide, there he was! On page 76 I saw a bigger-than-life illustration of a banded alder borer.

Yesterday as I ate my lunch on the front porch, the first butterfly of the season stopped to visit. He landed on my shirt, walked down my sleeve and across my hand. His excitement grew when he reached my fingertips. Traces of my cinnamon-covered graham cracker became lunch for him too. His long tongue licked while I studied his anatomy. When he flew away, I flew for my *Butterflies of North America* guidebook before I forgot his features. The dark, jagged edges of his orange wings, the black spots with a few white splashes, and the mottled underside identified this specimen as a California tortoiseshell.

This world fascinates me. Everywhere I look, some bug, flower, or mushroom shouts the glory of God to those who will take the time to listen.

Next time you go to a general bookstore, find the nature section. Pick up any field guide and flip through the pictures. Notice the colors, the shapes, and the sizes. Pick up the next one and do the same thing. Then try another, and another. After an hour, you've only begun to observe the multitudes of creatures on this planet. Who could have imagined such a variety of life-forms?

Jesus did. "For by him were all things created, that are in heaven, and that are in earth, visible and invisible..." (Colossians 1:16). Jesus, with unlimited imagination, unlimited power, and unlimited resources, created a visible world that displays the nature and glory of God. We have the senses to discover and observe these wonders. Whether we explore bugs, butterflies, or the far reaches of the universe, it's all amazing.

Two thousand years ago, this Creator, Jesus, limited Himself and became a man. He chose to lay aside His unrestrained position as God's equal and placed Himself within the confines of a human being. He bound Himself with gravity, time, and space (Philippians 2:2-11).

As a man, Jesus didn't make exotic animals and plants; however, He continued to create. During His thirty-three years in a human box, Jesus created a life that displayed God's attributes. He acted out love, forgiveness, mercy, and justice through the body of a carpenter from Nazareth. Near the close of this life He announced, "he that hath seen me hath seen the Father" (John 14:9). Jesus brought more glory to God while in the body of a human being than He did when He created the universe without any restraints. "Wherefore God also hath highly exalted him, and given him a name which is above every name: that at the name of Jesus every knee should bow, of things in heaven, and things in earth, and things under the earth; and that every tongue should confess that Jesus Christ is Lord, to the glory of God the Father."

The mystery of the ages is that Jesus dwells in people. Not only is He willing to put himself into the box of humanity, He willingly enters boxes called sinners—folks like you and me. When welcomed into a heart, Jesus grows and produces expressions of His Father.

Whosoever willingly surrenders his heart and soul to Jesus experiences this indwelling. Once there, Jesus keeps doing what He always does, creating wonders that honor God. The apostle Paul wrote, "But we have this treasure in earthen vessels, that the excellency of the power may be of God, and not of us" (2 Corinthians 4:7).

When a selfish, angry, and wicked-minded boy surrenders his wayward heart to this Treasure, God receives honor. As soon as Jesus prompts him to stop swearing, the boy obeys. His friends notice. When prompted to be gentle, the boy lays aside his rude temper and speaks kindly to his mother. She cannot help but see the change. His repentant life will become more of a wonder than that of a butterfly emerging from a cocoon. It's what happens when the Creator is free to make what He wants within the soul of a man.

"What will He do in me?" someone questions. None can tell, for His imagination is limitless. "But as it is written, Eye hath not seen, nor ear heard, neither have entered into the heart of man, the things which God hath prepared for them that love him" (1 Corinthians 2:9). Whatever He does within you will be as unique as the creatures found in any nature field guide.

You exist as a vessel to hold specific expressions of God. You're a display cabinet through which He shows His attributes. Nothing is worth having or doing if it clouds the exhibit Jesus wants to show.

What does this have to do with work?

Many men give their lives to careers. They work hard day after day trying to support a family, attempting to make ends meet. Some try to accomplish monumental tasks to prolong their names for generations to come. Men worry about getting jobs, going to school, and making decisions about the future.

All of this is insignificant when you consider that the One who created every bug, bird, animal, and star wants to use your body and soul to demonstrate His life each day. He wants the freedom to choose your jobs, to direct your path. Your life may seem as small as a matchbox. Who cares? The size of your box does not limit what Jesus might create in it.

Don't worry about your life work or your impact on the world. Your usefulness in life depends not on your talents, but upon the Treasure Who lives in your box.

Yield to Him and you'll be amazed at His imagination and creativity.

*But we have this treasure in earthen vessels, that
the excellency of the power may be of God,
and not of us.* (2 Corinthians 4:7)

Questions

• What type of beetle dresses like a basketball referee?

• Why did Jesus create the universe?

• What did Jesus display when He was in the form of a man?

• Why does Jesus want to dwell in people?

• Have you offered your heart to Jesus that He might create whatever He imagines in you?

Understanding Your Boss

In judging others a man labors in vain,
often errs and easily sins,
but in judging and examining himself,
he always labors fruitfully.

—Thomas à Kempis

Jack Hennen owned an irrigation and trenching company. Just before I turned twenty, Jack hired me to install underground telephone lines and sprinkling systems.

Arriving at the trenching shop one morning, Jack announced, "We got the job!"

"What job?" I asked.

"The Crescent Valley High School in Corvallis! We're low bidders on the irrigation and drainage systems. We start next month."

I began looking forward to the job. I liked driving. Working in Corvallis meant driving the company truck an hour north on old Highway 99, every day. I also liked the thought of our little company having such a big project.

At the high school I often worked alone on the future football field, baseball diamond, and among the shrubbery beds next to the classrooms. Occasionally Jack showed up and gave instructions for me and the part-time crew.

One crisp fall morning I started the trencher and headed across the soccer field. Jack told me to trench a grid of ditches for the water lines that fed sprinkler heads. The landscapers were putting pressure on us. They wanted all the underground work completed so they could level the dirt and sow the grass seed before the coming rains. I didn't want to be the one to hold them back.

Sitting on the operator's seat I kept an eye on the cutters behind me and another on the marker I aimed for on the far side of the barren field. Nobody could sneak up on me so I easily spotted the boss coming. I shut off the trencher.

After some small talk, he told me to stop what I was doing and go to the football field to install automatic water valves. I quit digging, gathered some tools, and walked to the football field. I was halfway finished with the first valve when Jack came out again and said, "Go back to trenching."

"What a waste," I thought. Picking up my tools I headed for the soccer field. Back on the trencher I looked up to see Jack coming again. "Hey Bob," he said, "I want you to go out to the football field and finish those valves."

I got mad and began arguing in my mind, "How could anything get done around here with a boss treating me like a yo-yo? Didn't he know that I could get twice as much done if he just left me alone for a while? Let me finish one job and I'll get to the other soon enough." The more I thought about it the madder I became.

I'm not proud of my attitude that day; I'm just giving you the brutal facts.

Employees tend to think they know more than the employers do. I thought so, especially when Jack jerked me around. "If only I was the boss," I thought, "then, we'd be productive!"

Later I learned that the landscapers planned to spread loam on the soccer field within three days. We *had* to have our lines in before then. That's why Jack put me on the trencher at the start of the day. The general contractor informed my boss that trucks were dumping dirt on the football field that afternoon. If we wanted to finish the valves before they were covered, we'd better do it quick. Therefore, Jack pulled me off the soccer field and started me on the valves. The trucking company said they couldn't be there for two days so he put me back on the soccer field. The general contractor told the trucking company, "They *would* begin dumping dirt no matter what!" Therefore, Jack ordered me back to the football field. What looked like foolish jerking was really my boss trying to do the most important job first. He had a good reason for it.

To me the boss looked like the fool, when in reality the fool was me. My limited understanding of the situation, my high opinion of my leadership abilities, and my low estimation of the boss's management skills got me into trouble. Even if my boss didn't know what he was doing, I lacked the proper Christian perspective.

Christians don't simply work for an earthly boss, they work for God. "Servants, obey in all things your masters according to the flesh; not with eyeservice, as menpleasers; but in singleness of heart, fearing God: And whatsoever ye do, do it heartily, as to the Lord, and not unto men" (Colossians 3:22,23). The mature Christian accepts his boss's commands as though they were God's commands. He purposes to do his work fully aware of his unseen Master.

The reality of a man's faith is tested by everyday events. Does he see an invisible God controlling the business world? Does he treat what his boss asks as God's will for him? It's Christian faith that believes the boss knows what he is doing, and if he doesn't know, God will still be honored by obedient work.

A wise Christian rejoices when promoted, because he knows God gave the promotion. He rejoices when demoted, for God designed that too. Whether you're hired or fired, God is in control. If you are lazy, God might prompt the boss to remove you. If you are diligent, He might move the boss to give you a raise. On the other hand, you might be a hardworking, diligent worker who is fired because God planned it. A working faith sees an unseen God in control of all.

Whether a ditch digger or a doctor, many men don't like their jobs. They are frustrated with their bosses, frustrated with government regulations, frustrated with other employees, frustrated with their hours, and frustrated with their pay. A Christian has no excuse for this frustration. The basis of Christianity is faith that God controls life. He could change all your circumstances if He wanted to. He sets the stage of our lives and continually attends to every detail.

Jesus said that He came to do the will of His Father. The Father's will put Him under the authority of a phony religious system and a corrupt government. The Father willed to use these "authorities" to kill His Son. God controlled every second of Jesus' life. Every authority over Him, every limitation, and every opportunity were designed by God to best display His love through Jesus. God is just as much in control of your life, including your boss and your job.

If the god you claim to serve does not rule over the world, if you cannot trust him to direct the hearts of kings, to oversee every army, to attend to everything that pertains to your life, you had better get a different god. Quit working for a weakling and get a job serving the True God that created you.

If you murmur and dispute about your earthly boss, you betray yourself. You announce that you don't have a God Who leads you down the best path. You announce that you don't believe "that all things work together for good to them that love God, to them who are the called according to his purpose" which is "to be conformed to the image of his Son" (Romans 8:28,29).

You will understand your earthly boss only when you understand that your Heavenly Boss controls all bosses and gives His best to you through each one.

> **The king's heart is in the hand of the LORD,**
> **as the rivers of water: he turneth it**
> **whithersoever he will.** (Proverbs 21:1)

Questions

- My boss's direction looked foolish to me. Was it?

- Do bosses have to tell their employees why they do things?

- What truth will allow an employee to remain content even when his boss is asking him to do what looks foolish?

- Do you believe that God controls the hearts of bosses and only gives you what is best through them?

Unemployed?

Have thy tools ready:
God will find thee work.

—Charles Kingsley

I stood in the middle of a slow-moving employment line. Everyone said that I deserved to receive unemployment compensation and the papers in my hands proved it. I felt out of place, but I couldn't put my finger on why. Was I really without a job? Did I want government aid?

As I argued with myself, a small voice spoke in my heart. "Do you work for Me?" my God quietly asked.

"Yes," I answered.

"Is there nothing to do in My kingdom?"

"There is plenty of work in Your kingdom," I replied.

"Then why are you standing in this line?"

That was a good question. I stepped out of line, took my papers to a clerk and said, "I'm not unemployed." Then I turned and walked out. Since then, I've never been without useful work, and I've always had food and clothing.

A Christian man will always have a job. Our God will always provide what we need. Our work is to believe Him, to hear His voice, and to obey what we hear. He may lead us into a business career and He may as easily lead us out of it. Our work is not a moneymaking position we hold. Our work is following Him.

As I walked out of the government office I asked, "What do I do now?" Many things came to my mind. My mom needed help around her house. I knew a few widows with needs. Often my paid positions prevented me from being useful; now I had plenty of time.

I began helping folks, especially those who couldn't pay. The projects were often simple: a stuck door, a clogged gutter, or yard work. People unable to pay for the work they needed openly showed their gratefulness. Though they had little money, they often were good cooks. A tasty lunch with a person who was hungry for conversation made for satisfying meals.

God continued to meet my needs though it wasn't through a regular paycheck. One widow entered an old shed and returned with some tools that belonged to her late husband. "Please take these. They are of no use to me." She gave me a sledgehammer and various other useful tools. They were worth a day's wages and after twenty-five years, I still use the hammer.

That year I worked for ten widows, each with limited resources. In December, when my family began to feel the strain from lack of funds, I began to question my ways. Was I foolishly too generous? But in spite of my questioning, God knew where He sent me each day and knew what I needed.

West Coast Steel hired me that month to lay decking in a mile-long conveyor belt system for a mining company in Montana. We built bridge-like sections here in Eugene and shipped them to the mine. The company invited me to their Christmas party. When I opened their Christmas card, $2200 fell out! We finished that year well paid.

As an independent contractor, I never know how much money will come in during a month. I know that it will always be what we need. The challenge is to be on the *right* job, not to be on *a* job. Often we think that we are on the right job if we make the most money. That's not always true. If job A will net $25 today and job B will gain me $300, which job should I take? If I consistently take job B, I may be working for money instead of working for God. "No man can serve two masters: for either he will hate the one, and love the other; or else he will hold to the one, and despise the other. Ye cannot serve God and mammon" (Matthew 6:24). We have all heard that verse from the Bible, yet we Americans are constantly on the verge of serving money as our god. Our culture worships money, and I am afraid it influences us more than we realize. If God has called us to serve a particular person or to provide a service for our community that pays well, do it. On the other hand, if we are always looking for some situation to provide the most money for ourselves, we must beware of serving mammon.

My calling is to serve God by building houses and homes. It's easy to build a house, and more challenging to build a home. Building houses requires alertness to changing building codes and learning to use new tools and products. Building homes requires an open heart toward God, orderliness in my own home, and growth in understanding family relations.

When I have no houses to build, I ask myself, "If I knew that next Monday I would begin a new house project, what would I do today to get ready for it?" I sharpen my chisels, restock my screw bins, and fix the cord on the drill. I might catch up on any paperwork or wash the truck. Many times as soon as I get ready for an imaginary job, it comes. I'm ready to start immediately.

I use the same mentality in building homes. When there are no fathers to encourage, or no pressing needs to meet, I prepare for them. Maybe I'll read the Bible looking for answers to particular questions that fathers ask. I might gather other helpful resources. It doesn't bother me when there are no houses or no homes to build. Building runs in cycles, feast or famine they call it. I want to prepare for the feast while in the middle of the famine. The dinner always comes.

My own family and house get extra attention when jobs are in a lull. (I say extra attention, because families always need regular attention.) Again, I say to myself, "Soon I will be very busy. What should I do now that I won't have time for tomorrow?" Maybe I should get gravel for the driveway or till the garden. I try to work at home as hard as I would on a construction site, to accomplish what I won't have time for when future responsibilities arrive.

By listening to God's voice and responding in obedience, a man fulfills all that his True Boss requires of him. That Boss will certainly supply the needs of His workers.

There's no room for slothfulness. Many men experience financial trouble, not because God hasn't given them the resources, but because they have squandered what He has given. There is a season for everything, and a man cannot afford to sleep in the harvest. An undisciplined man experiences shortages in his heart and wallet.

Hard, diligent, and timely work is a man's calling. However, don't fall into the trap of simply working for money. Our goal is to yield ourselves as servants to God. He's not worried about money, and His promise to meet our necessities is sure. Money is a lifeless object. It cannot meet a fraction of our needs, though it makes a false appearance of doing so. God provides for our needs. He may use money, but He is never limited to it.

If you have no money-making job at hand, or even in sight, don't worry about it. You don't work for money. A Christian works for God.

If that statement seems too idealistic and unpractical, if it seems out of touch with the real world, you haven't come to know the God Who created you. It's not only practical but it's the road to freedom from the drudgery, fear, and the weariness of trying to earn a living.

God reserves for Himself the right to direct you as He wishes. He may choose to take you out of money-making employment for years. On the other hand, He might put you in a factory all your life. The position isn't an issue. Our response to God is.

If God is your boss, money comes and flies away without emotional attachment. He may provide your needs through diligent work at a paying job or from some place you never imagined. The point is: He meets your need. Your job is to believe and obey Him. That occupation is always available and gives the best return for your time.

Get to work!

Then said they unto him, What shall we do, that we might work the works of God?
Jesus answered and said unto them, This is the work of God, that ye believe on him whom he hath sent.
(John 6:28,29)

Questions

- As a Christian, what is our work?

- Does that job ever end?

- What happens if you try to serve God and money at the same time?

- If someone always takes the lesser paying job, does that mean he is serving God?

- What did Jesus mean when He said that our work was to believe in God?

Vision

A vision without a task is but a dream
A task without a vision is drudgery
A task with a vision is the hope of the world.

—Inscription on a church in England, 1730

Don needed a two-by-four, nine inches long. Grabbing a ten-inch block, he measured nine inches, set his square on the edge and drew a straight line across the board with his pencil. Then he reached for a Skilsaw to make the cut.

What was Don doing wrong? If you know, you have vision. If not, you are blind in this particular area of life. His actions were serious enough that if he worked for me, I would have yelled at him. It would not be the time to speak quietly.

Don pulled the trigger on the saw and began to cut. Small blocks are hard to hold. The saw blade bound in the wood. Faster than you can imagine, the block spun into the blade. Don had a tight grip on the two-by-four. When the wood jerked into the saw so did his thumb. All three dropped to the ground: saw, block, and thumb.

Skilsaws are great tools. I've used them to build many houses, but not to cut little blocks. If the board is less than fourteen inches, I won't hold it in one hand and cut with the other. It's too dangerous. I either clamp it to a sawhorse or get a longer board. It's better to waste some lumber than my thumb.

If you didn't know before, now you understand: don't cut small blocks with a Skilsaw! Now you know why I would have yelled at Don if I had caught him trying it on my job. You've gained vision.

Vision is the ability to see future events. It connects what you are doing now with what will happen later. It also links what you are about to do with something you have seen in the past. When Don needs a nine-inch board and he sees a ten-inch block, his *vision* will see a thumb on the ground. I hope that vision will keep him, and you, from repeating the same mistake.

A worker with vision avoids trouble and saves huge amounts of money. If a roofer imagines someone standing on the ground below him, he'll look over the edge and holler before he throws off scrap roofing. A heavy-equipment operator checks the oil in his machine each morning because he can imagine what happens to an engine that runs without lubrication. The ability to picture water spraying thirty feet into the sky prompts an excavator to call the underground locating company *before* he begins digging. An employee who looks ahead and sees the potential consequences of his actions is valuable to any company.

Companies want experienced workers because vision comes from experience. Experience comes from making mistakes. Part of training a new employee is anticipating that he will make almost every mistake possible. I constantly keep one eye on him for his safety and mine. Each time he makes and corrects an error, I become more relaxed. Most guys seem to remember their blunders more than my instructions.

As the boss, I usually pay for my employee's mistakes. Therefore, I ask myself, "Do I need him enough to risk damaging my tools, my truck, the materials, himself, and me?" If I'm convinced he is worth more than what I'm likely to lose, I'll hire him.

Sometimes I'll hire a young man just because I want to invest in him as a person. In that case, I pay the price without hope of financial return. The worth is in seeing a young man develop.

For these reasons, don't be frustrated when a company requires experience before they'll hire you. It's really vision that they want, and often they can't afford to hire someone without it.

Vision not only avoids errors, it motivates men to work. Many mornings I've rolled out of bed exhausted, wishing I could sleep another hour. The vision of my wife and children pushes me to provide food and shelter for them. I may not feel like writing a letter, but a picture in my mind of a discouraged friend leads me to pick up my pen and write words of hope.

"Where there is no vision, the people perish..." (Proverbs 29:18). Without the ability to see into the future a man is at risk. He's blind to approaching danger and ignorant of great opportunities. He is like a blindfolded boxer who can't see where to punch and hasn't a clue from where he was hit.

How does a young man gain vision? One way is hindsight. Hindsight is looking at what just happened to you. Like the time the city boy touched the electric fence after being told not to. It knocked him to the ground. *Yeeeooouuchhhh!* He gained a vision of what electric fences can do. When you make a mistake, learn from it.

I've never met a perfect worker; we all make errors. However, a man might reduce his mistakes and gain vision by watching others. Observing and avoiding the errors of others tends to make your education less painful.

The second half of this proverb describes another source of vision, "Where there is no vision, the people perish: but he that keepeth the law, happy is he" (Proverbs 29:18). I bought a new six-inch jointer for my wood shop. Rule number eleven on the safety chart warns, "Never joint or plane any material less than 10 inches long." If I don't have the vision to know what happens while attempting to joint a small block, obeying rule eleven protects me.

Every new power tool comes with an owner's manual. Each manual begins with a statement like this: *"For your own safety, read instruction manual before operating the tool. Failure to follow these rules may result in serious personal injury."* The manufacturer hopes to give buyers a vision of what the tool can and cannot do. This insight allows the operator to get the most work out of the machine with the least damage to himself.

More than any manufacturer, God wants to protect us from damage. Therefore, He gave us the Bible. It contains rules that we may not understand because we lack His vision. A wise man obeys what he sees in that Book, even if he doesn't understand why. In time, experience will open his eyes.

Besides obeying the Bible yourself, watch what others do and consider the consequences of their actions. By comparing what you see in life to what the Bible says, your vision will improve.

The world desperately needs men with vision. Not just men that can keep their hands out of a Skilsaw, but men who can see ahead to dangers others are unaware of.

As you develop the foresight to avoid cutting off your fingers with a saw, you make steps toward developing the eyesight to be a leader in your community and nation. Perhaps some day your vision will allow you to build sturdy houses, peaceful homes, and help lead those around you from danger on the paths of life.

But blessed are your eyes, for they see:
and your ears, for they hear. (Matthew 13:16)

Questions

- What is vision?

- What did Don fail to see?

- Name three ways to gain vision.

- If you lose your vision, what is one way to still keep out of trouble?

- Why do employers want vision in their employees?

What Are You Going to Do?

Our main business is not to see what lies dimly at a distance, but to do what lies clearly at hand.

—Thomas Carlyle

Has anyone ever asked you, "What are you going to do when you grow up?" Does the thought of choosing a vocation leave you feeling nervous? Can you confidently decide a course of study and training with the assurance it's the best for you?

Our society puts pressure upon young folks to know their future and have a plan to reach it. After over fifty years of living, I still don't know what I'll be doing next year.

Twelve months ago, I never imagined that this summer I would be training boys to build a house. God imagined it. He began preparing me over thirty years ago, when I took a job pounding nails for $2.50 an hour. I saw it as the first job I could find. He saw it as a training ground for His future plans.

We can't see into the future, but God can. Little things that seem unimportant to us today are essential parts of God's plan for tomorrow. If we neglect little things by focusing on doing big things, we miss valuable training designed to make us useful in God's Kingdom.

Just as an employer will train his workers to perform a job, God trains His people by the events He brings into their lives, "I will instruct thee and teach thee in the way which thou shalt go: I will guide thee with mine eye" (Psalm 32:8).

The frustration of trying to see into the future vanishes when we simply trust the One Who controls life. We don't have to be nervous, fearful, or always wondering if we are making the right choices. If we relax and put our best effort into what comes, He will surely make us into useful servants.

Our first, God-designed classroom is our home. He knows what kind of people our parents are. If you have only a father, only a mother or neither, He understands. In this setting, you have important lessons to learn, and God is your personal tutor. *Whatever work you have at home, put your whole heart into it. God will use it to lead you into a relationship with Himself and prepare you for future opportunities.* I've emphasized this statement. You would do well to highlight it, circle it, and never forget it.

Seeing home assignments as the training ground for your life is so basic most people overlook it. They tend to want something more glamorous. Let's face it. Most of us don't know what we want to do in life. Neither are we wise enough to tell the difference between the good and the best things to do. If we would simply yield to what God brings to us each day and put our whole heart and soul into it, we'll be ready for each position we face in life.

Amerigo Vespucci (1451-1512) claimed to have discovered the continent of South America in 1497. He was a young man who put his heart into whatever he did. When exposed to astronomy, he learned all he could. He began working as a merchant because his relatives gave him a job. Applying himself to each task, Amerigo received promotions and more responsibilities. His merchant training opened the door to join a company fitting ships for long voyages. The opportunity came to take a voyage himself. He accepted. His astronomy skills exceeded everyone else's on the ship, opening the door to become a navigator. Before long, he managed a number of vessels. During this time, he explored the South American coast. The king of Spain learned of his navigational skills and appointed Vespucci as the nation's chief pilot, training all other navigators.

There seem to be some contradictions among the biographers of Amerigo Vespucci. However, all agree that he accepted each opportunity placed before him and applied himself, with a single heart, to learn what he could. Who would have imagined that what began as faithful work for a merchant relative would end leaving his name on world maps five hundred years later? Being famous isn't the goal, being faithful is. Those who are diligent in little things stand before kings one day.

Who would have imagined that David, the son of Jesse, would learn to be a great warrior and a king by taking care of his father's animals?

Jesse had a few sheep in the wilderness. He assigned his son to feed them. In this shepherd's classroom, David learned to be "cunning in playing [a musical instrument], and a mighty valiant man, and a man of war, and prudent in matters, and a comely person" (1 Samuel 16:18). How did David learn all these things by being a shepherd? He simply put his heart into taking care of his dad's sheep.

If David had complained about his position, neglected the sheep, and rejected work at home for a more favorable situation, he would have been rejecting God's personal training.

By prompting Jesse to make his son a shepherd, God arranged a setting where He could personally train David, alone in the wilderness. He picked one day to send a bear after a sheep. He chose another time to bring a lion. He taught David about birth and death, leading and following, and tenderness and compassion. David needed an unconventional education because God wanted an unconventional warrior and king.

When God wanted to slay Goliath, He prompted Jesse to send David to visit his brothers on the battlefield. God wanted a simple youth, skillful in slinging rocks to defy the armies of the Philistines in the name of the Lord. David was His man.

When God desired a good king to rule His people, "He chose David…his servant, and took him from the sheepfolds: From following the ewes great with young he brought him to feed Jacob his people, and Israel his inheritance." David was ready. "So he fed them according to the integrity of his heart; and guided them by the skilfulness of his hands" (Psalm 78:70-72).

God's classroom for David worked because David willingly accepted an everyday job at home with his whole heart.

Are you accepting the classrooms God has picked for you? Do you see your assignments around home as opportunities to develop unconventional skills that will one day fit you for God's unconventional tasks? You don't need to know what you will do in the future. By faith you can confidently trust that you'll be prepared for it. You may need to take some classes in the future to learn specific skills. However, your heart to work, your vision, and your basic outlook upon life is formed by how you accept the daily assignments you currently have at your home.

If you are serious about becoming an unconventional man, trained by our Creator, ask your parents or guardians, "What things do you wish I would do around here?" and then accomplish their desires with all your heart.

A twenty-year-old friend named Andrew came to visit me this week. Like many young people, he experiences depression and discouragement from time to time. He told me the past week had been the happiest week of his life.

"What made the change?" I asked.

He told me that he set out to do what he knew his parents wanted him to do. When they left for work, he began by cleaning the kitchen and continued into other areas of the house. Then he went outside and mowed the lawn. When his parents returned in the evening, they were happy. I wish you could have seen the smile on his face as he told me the story.

Andrew wants to walk in God's ways. He found that accepting the care of his parents' home as a special training assignment lifted him out of depression, brought joy to his whole house, and gave him an awareness of God's presence all day long.

How is housework going to fit Andrew for God's call on his life? I don't know how, but it will. Who will do better in life, a discouraged young man or one who cheerfully develops skills and vision by making his home a better place to live?

Regardless of your age or circumstances, if you put your heart into the daily things before you, God will develop His heart within you. You'll be under special training to fit you perfectly for a useful role in the future. It doesn't really matter what you will become. Set your sights on doing what you should today. The rest will fall in line.

The next time someone asks you, "What are you going to do in the future?" you can look them in the eye and confidently answer, "I don't know what the future holds. However, I know that by being faithful with the little things I need to do today, I'll be ready for it when it comes."

Trust in the LORD with all thine heart; and lean not
unto thine own understanding.
In all thy ways acknowledge him, and
he shall direct thy paths. (Proverbs 3:5,6)

Questions

• What is the first classroom God prepares for us?

• What is one of the best ways to develop skills for the future?

• How did God prepare David to be a warrior and king?

• What made Andrew say that the past week was one of the happiest in his life?

• What quality in Amerigo Vespucci set him up for greatness?

When Mercy Goes to Work

Good for good is only fair,
Bad for bad soon brings despair,
Bad for good is vile and base,
Good for bad shows forth God's grace.

—Welsh saying

Of all God's attributes, my favorite is His mercy. God displays His mercy by His desire to bring all the good He can imagine upon every person who has ever wronged Him.

Mercy requires offenders. You might be kind and gracious to nice folks. However, to show mercy, one must first have an offender. Once wronged you are then free to show mercy by tempering justice, overlooking injuries, or treating the rascal better than he deserves.

If you stand in Sisters, Oregon and look west, the ground before you is relatively flat. Few people notice that ground because just past it, seven major mountain peaks rise majestically into the sky. They're an inspiration to all who see them because they are so big and beautiful. God's mercy is like that. "Let the wicked forsake his way, and the unrighteous man his thoughts: and let him return unto the LORD, and he will have mercy upon him; and to our God, for he will abundantly pardon. For my thoughts are not your thoughts, neither are your ways my ways, saith the LORD. For as the heavens are higher than the earth, so are my ways higher than your ways, and my thoughts than your thoughts" (Isaiah 55:7-9).

God's mercy draws my heart, like the Cascade Mountains draw my eyes. My tendency is to be good to those who are good to me, and to neglect those who wrong me. God is above that. He's good not only to the just, but also to the unjust.

The Bible makes it clear that God's ways are higher than the ordinary lives of men and then commands us to be like Him, "Be ye therefore merciful, as your Father also is merciful" (Luke 6:36). How can that be? Isn't that asking too much? It is not asking too much. Genuine Christianity is much more than ordinary living, and God wants to draw us into it.

We need two things to lift us out of the common life of getting upset with offenders and into a beautiful life of mercy. One is a heart that obeys God's promptings. The other is somebody to offend us. For you can't display mercy unless somebody does you wrong.

If you are one of those fortunate ones who gets tricked out of your money, who receives rude comments from your friends, and who is treated poorly by people who don't understand what you are doing, be glad! Thank God for the chance to live in the mountains of His mercy.

If you don't thank God for each opportunity to be merciful, you'll probably respond like most folks, with cruelty. You don't have to be a ruthless dictator to be considered cruel. Every one of us has a mean streak.

Suppose you see the local bully riding his bike toward you. As you step off the sidewalk to give him room, he rides by, reaches out his hand, and knocks the notebook from your arms. Laughing, he looks over his shoulder at your papers flying in the breeze. He fails to notice the low bus-stop sign hanging over the walkway. Looking back at you with a smirk on his face, he runs the side of his head into that sign. Smack! The bike keeps going until it runs into a trash can. The bully is face down, wondering what happened.

Did you feel a faint smile coming on as I told that story? A cruel person will think it's funny and that the bully had it coming. On the other hand, a merciful person's first thought is concern for his head. Which are you?

Cruel people imagine ways to get even with offenders. They laugh to themselves when an enemy trips. They hold grudges and refuse to do them good. These folks also don't experience God as they could, because His ways are higher than their ways and His thoughts higher than their thoughts. They travel on a different road than God travels.

As a general building contractor, God gives me many opportunities each day to participate in His desire to bring mercy to offenders. I can choose whether to walk the high road in fellowship with Him or the low road selfishly alone. When somebody stole four thousand dollars' worth of tools from my truck, when the electrician never showed up when he said he would, when the floor layer charged twice the estimated cost, when the homeowner didn't keep his promise, when the salesman flat out lied: these are all opportunities to walk with God in His mercy.

If a man doesn't find enough chances for mercy on a job, just live in a family for a week. Brothers and sisters, parents and children provide many great situations to express mercy.

Besides jobs and families, there is one more place to show mercy—dealing with a governmental agency. I mention these three places because God works in families where relationships are closest, in marketplaces wherever people exchange goods and services, and in governments where one person rules over another. These are set stages to act out mercy, and you have a leading role.

The excitement of Christian living is in participating with God while He works. He may show Himself in meetings and assemblies, but most often He displays Himself in common life, in daily business where people interact with each other. Keep alert during these events and you'll discover countless opportunities to exercise mercy.

Miserable people fill much of the workplaces in America today. Many think their bosses give them a raw deal. Some feel their fellow employees don't do their part. Others are sure they don't get the respect they deserve. You can bring God's love into these messes if you are willing to look past injuries and trespasses to acts of kindness.

Jesus, Who is always the standard, entered a world of miserable people with a heart to save. They had rejected His Father. Walking in immorality, they loved themselves and hated everyone else. He could have condemned, but instead He brought mercy. There were none good, not even one, yet He came with the desire to benefit them all.

This lesson on mercy is not easy. One day, I set out to show mercy to everyone that crossed me. Instead of giving mercy, I found myself cruel and wanting to get even with my offenders. I knew what was right, but my heart didn't want to do it. The day's adventures exposed my cruel heart, leaving me discouraged and ashamed of myself.

I remembered what Jesus said, "Abide in me, and I in you. As the branch cannot bear fruit of itself, except it abide in the vine; no more can ye, except ye abide in me. I am the vine, ye are the branches: He that abideth in me, and I in him, the same bringeth forth much fruit: for without me ye can do nothing" (John 15:4,5). God doesn't give assignments for us to run off to accomplish alone. He wants to do it together. This is a secret to the abundant Christian life.

When pride tells you that you have a good heart, it's a shock to learn the truth that in reality it's cruel, yet this is a step toward experiencing God. The following day, instead of self-confidently setting out to be merciful, I had to confess, "Father, You are merciful and I am cruel. When I try on my own, I fall short. Will You live Your mercy through me today, to love the folks that wrong me. Without You, there is no hope for me."

God wants to take our weak and willing hearts and work through them in our homes, jobs, and government. Instead of us withdrawing in anger when offended, He'll teach us to welcome each offense as an opportunity. We'll become vessels carrying God's mercy to hurting people.

The chance of a lifetime, the prospect of being merciful as our Father in heaven is merciful, is waiting for us. By His power, we can be men who love our enemies, who bless those that curse us, who do good to them that hate us, and who pray for them which despite-fully use us.

The next time someone offends you, let God fill you with His forgiving heart. Let mercy go to work with you, and your soul will never be the same again.

The merciful man doeth good to his own soul:
but he that is cruel troubleth his own flesh.
(Proverbs 11:17)

Questions

• What is mercy?

• Why can't you be merciful to someone who does good to you?

• Why does God ask us to be merciful?

• Where do you get the ability to show mercy?

• Why should we rejoice when someone offends us?

You're Rude

Two men looked through prison bars,
the one saw mud, the other stars.

Last week Floyd and I installed trim in a new two-story office building full of tiny rooms. The office spaces were so small we could hardly set up our saws to cut the materials. Floyd set up his in a narrow back hallway. If he cut a long board to the left of the blade, it extended into a closet. If it went to the right, it stuck out the back door and onto the city sidewalk. Crowded in a maze of halls and cramped by piles of baseboard and casing, we struggled to give the owners a good job.

Into the building walked two painters. The plump boss, chewing on a toothpick, led the way. His skinny helper followed. They stuck their noses into each little office, systematically considering every corner both upstairs and down.

"What are you guys doing?" asked Floyd.

"We're gonna paint the balusters for the hand rail," the boss man answered.

"Don't you have a shop where you can take them?" Floyd asked.

"No."

"How about another job you're doing? Can't you take them there?"

"No."

They grunted and mumbled between themselves, walking around until they settled in an upstairs southern room and began masking the walls. Indifferent to our questions and dumb looks that said, "I don't believe you are actually doing what it looks like you're about to do," they began spraying oil-based primer on the balusters.

The wind blew strongly from the south. When they opened their window to get fresh air, they got plenty. The same wind that gave them clean air spread the paint fumes throughout the whole office building.

Floyd and I felt like we had stuck our faces into a can of paint. Before we could grab a few of our most expensive tools and get out of the door, we both had headaches.

I know that God is merciful. His mind is full of kindness for offenders. I know that He wants me to be merciful like Him…but those painters weren't just offensive, they were downright rude, not to mention thoughtless, selfish, and inconsiderate.

My spirit kept saying to me, "Cheer up; be merciful; do something good for them." However, my mind rejected the promptings and stubbornly held their offenses against them. I didn't want to be nice to them, talk to them, or even look at them.

My mind was full of two self-centered painters. I imagined what miserable relationships they must have, if they had any at all. Why would a builder hire such creeps?

As Floyd and I staggered to our trucks, we lamented about our headaches, said a short good-bye, and headed home.

I had traveled over an hour to work that day and it seemed like a waste to go home early. The long drive was good for me though. It gave me time to think.

As I drove along, my spirit and my mind continued to battle it out. "Be merciful," my spirit would say. "I can't believe how rude they were," my mind complained. After some time my mind recalled a secret of life that has pulled me out of many troubles. It's simple.

The secret was this: "In every thing give thanks: for this is the will of God in Christ Jesus concerning you" (1 Thessalonians 5:18). Somewhere on the freeway between Brownsville and Coburg my mind gave up the fight and said, "Thank You, God, for bringing those painters today."

Immediately, I let the painter's offenses go. I turned to God and began seeing the good that rude painters can bring. One benefit was that I'd be home early in the evening and could spend more time with my family. Another was driving in daylight. Though I could think up many blessings, the best came as God spoke to my heart something like this:

"You have often acted just like those painters. You've come onto jobs thinking that you own the place. Just because you were building the staircase in the front entry, you thought you could barge in and push other workers to the back of the house. You haven't always stopped to consider their needs. You've put yourself first." He gave me enough examples from my past to drive the lesson home and continued to instruct me, "Now you know what other subcontractors feel like when you carelessly push them around. I sent those painters today. Rude? Yes. Thoughtless? Yes. At times you've acted just like them—insensitive to others and focusing on your job alone."

I felt like God had gently put His arm around me. He pulled me to Himself and with great kindness exposed my wrongs. It wasn't a spanking, though I deserved one. It was my Father giving me instruction. He used the wayward actions of a couple of painters to show me my faults. He gave me the opportunity to see the practical good that comes from a thankful heart.

I didn't feel grateful when I first gave thanks for those painters. However, at that point, everything changed. The whole situation made me want to think about others on the job. It made me want to be kind. But best of all, my thoughts were released from concentrating on the ugly side of life to considering God. Choosing to be thankful brought me out of complaining into joy.

God has given us everything we'll ever need to walk successfully through life. Peter told us, "According as his divine power hath given unto us all things that pertain unto life and godliness...that by these ye might be partakers of the divine nature, having escaped the corruption that is in the world through lust"(2 Peter 1:3,4). You can have a grateful heart if you want one. God offers one to any person who simply chooses to be thankful. It lifts us out of useless thoughts and brings upon us God's joyful presence.

Everyday business is the perfect place for thankfulness. If you have a self-centered boss, rude customers, and inconsiderate fellow workers, thank God for them. He handpicks these folks for you. Maybe these people are mirrors of our own ugly hearts that prompt us to call out to God for mercy. Perhaps they are the ones God will use to teach us valuable life lessons. You cannot imagine all the benefits that await you if you genuinely thank God for bringing inconsiderate people into your life.

You choose whether you'll live your days upset with offenders, or whether you'll abide in the pleasure of God's presence. How you'll spend your days depends on whether you'll accept this simple guide to life: "In everything give thanks."

*Giving thanks always for all things
unto God and the Father in the name of our Lord
Jesus Christ.* (Ephesians 5:20)

Questions

- Why did I get upset with the painters?

- What tool did God give me to get out of my trouble?

- Name two things that happen when you give thanks for troubles and trials.

- Why is everyday business a good place to practice thankfulness?

- How does God use people as a mirror for our faults?

Work Within the Rules

It is much safer to obey than to rule.

—Thomas à Kempis

I like trucks, especially big trucks. They attract me like a magnet attracts iron filings. As a little boy, trucks delighted me, but washing log trucks as a teenager hooked me for life.

I liked the feel of driving those rigs around the parking lot and into the wash pit. The big steering wheels, sitting high above the pavement, and shifting gears thrilled me. After an hour of washing, I'd climb up into the cab and sit on the floating leather seat. Turning the key, waiting for the glow plugs, and feeling the engine rumble to life made me feel like the captain of an enormous ship. When the air compressor filled the brake lines, I'd find my gear, ease off the clutch, and begin to roll.

Sometimes I got up enough speed to shift into second gear while crossing the parking lot, but usually I just let the truck slowly lumber back to its space.

Once there, I'd back in parallel to the trucks on both sides and stop with the front bumper exactly in line with the others. *Chewwwwww.* That was the noise of air releasing when I pulled the parking brake. A flip of the engine switch and the truck rattled to a stop. I'd jump to the ground, slam the door, and run around to climb up into the next one.

Though I only washed trucks for a year, the desire to be around them seemed to get into my blood. I can't drive Interstate 5 without turning my head to check out an old Peterbilt or Mack.

Ray had trucks in his blood too. He was my neighbor during the early 1980s when paying jobs were scarce. With money his grandmother gave him, Ray bought an old Freightliner truck and trailer. He began hauling freight between Seattle and Los Angeles.

Ray seldom came home. He rushed up and down the West Coast delivering steel, lumber, and any other load he could find. Whenever I saw him, he looked as worn out as the retreads on his trailer.

One Saturday morning while he worked on the engine, I went out to visit with Ray. He lamented how hard it was to make a living driving a truck. The cost of fuel, engine maintenance, and tire repairs took everything he made.

Ray said that he had to drive sixteen hours each day to pay for his truck and his family's expenses. Federal law regulates how long a driver can stay at the wheel each day and how many hours he can drive during a week. Truckers keep a logbook to record their driving time. They must have it current and available for police officers and weigh masters to inspect. One purpose is to keep sleepy drivers off the road. Ray tried to avoid these laws and fool the authorities by keeping two separate logbooks. "Everyone does it," he said. "To compete, I have to cheat."

To compete, Ray began doing other things, like taking drugs to keep awake. The pressure to protect Grandma's investment and to feed his family pushed him to try anything, legal or not.

The day came when Ray couldn't make the truck payments. He lost the truck, the borrowed money, and even his wife. The last I heard, Ray was broke and living with his grandmother.

If you have to work illegally to make ends meet, find something else to do. God understands bureaucracy. He knows all about the laws men make. He is wise enough to work profitably within those rules, to change the rules, or to lead you to a different job.

God warned His people through the prophet Jeremiah, "As the partridge sitteth on eggs, and hatcheth them not; so he that getteth riches, and not by right, shall leave them in the midst of his days, and at his end shall be a fool" (Jeremiah 17:11). The warning applies to us today. Ray showed a living example of trying to make money by cheating. He met a fool's end.

No matter what your goal may be, if you have to cheat to get it, it's not worth having. It's better to be penniless than to possess anything you stole or swindled to get. When you use illegal methods to get what you want, you've rejected God and are using the wisdom of fools.

On the other hand, "Blessed is the man that trusteth in the Lord, and whose hope the Lord is." If you want to see God work, let your refusal to cheat put you in a place where unless God saves you, you're lost. God loves to rescue people who throw away their own schemes and put their trust in Him.

When Jesus and His disciples entered Capernaum, the tribute collectors approached Peter and asked if his master paid tribute. As the Creator of the universe, Jesus didn't owe tribute money to anyone. However, when He chose to become a man and take on the form of a servant, He also chose to obey the rules of the Roman government. The whole situation was a set-up to display His gentleness and power to provide.

Jesus told Peter, "lest we should offend them, go thou to the sea, and cast an hook, and take up the fish that first cometh up; and when thou hast opened his mouth, thou shalt find a piece of money: that take, and give unto them for me and thee" (Matthew 17:27).

The ever-increasing laws and requirements of the world's governments and our limited resources are opportunities to display the Father, just as Jesus did. It's the Christian's privilege to respond gently to the demands of civil authorities and to trust God's miraculous provisions. Those who yield to unjust governmental rules are often surprised how God supplies their need. It may not be through catching a coin-eating fish, yet often His provisions are just as miraculous.

Whether you drive trucks or sit in an accounting office, everyday business overflows with rules and regulations that provide opportunities for God to show His gentle, generous nature. If you grumble and cheat your way around them, you miss the chance to see Him work. Instead of experiencing God's timely provisions and leading, all you get is your own discontented self.

However, if you obey God when He says, "call upon me in the day of trouble: I will deliver thee, and thou shalt glorify me" (Psalm 50:15), you will experience how your God meets your need, exactly when you need it.

A Christian doesn't obey rules only because it is the right thing to do. He obeys because of the joy he receives from seeing his living God work in everyday situations.

When governments become bigger and more dominating, the Christian worker does not have to worry. He can relax. Governments are never stronger than God, because they get their power from Him. Therefore, no administration will ever tie His hands from miraculously delivering His people in their time of need. That doesn't mean that things will always be easy. However, you may have confidence that every event in life, even the government, is under the watchful eye of God. Unless the rules demand that you deny Him, work within them.

Instead of fighting and struggling your way through life, instead of resenting the laws of governments, I hope you develop the courage and faith to see restrictions as opportunities for God to show Himself real.

God is big enough to work within the rules that little men make. Don't miss the joy of His presence because you're busy whining about overbearing regulations.

May you have the courage to comply with quietness and confidence. For there you'll find your strength and your God.

Let every soul be subject unto the higher powers.
For there is no power but of God: the powers that be
are ordained of God. (Romans 13:1)

Questions

- Why did Ray meet a fool's end?

- What could he have done differently?

- Did Jesus need to pay the tribute?

- Why did He pay it?

- Why doesn't God worry about oppressive governments?

Finish It

Whatever a youth undertakes to learn, he should
not be suffered to leave it until he can reach his
arms round it and clench his hands on the other
side. Thus he will learn the habit of thoroughness.

—Samuel Smiles

This summer a man hired me to build a house. He asked if I would use three of his sons as my crew. I remember that day in June when we began. I opened the doors to the back of my truck exposing a pile of tools. The boys stood there, Nathan (14), Paul (12), and Davey (8), wondering what to do next.

All summer they have arrived at seven each morning ready for the day. Now, when I pull up to the job and open the back doors, they begin grabbing tools and spreading them around preparing for work.

Together we have framed the house and are now installing the siding. They've learned to run electric saws, pneumatic guns, and all kinds of useful tools. We have filled in many gaps in their knowledge of construction methods and building materials. It has been a great experience working side by side, turning lumber into a house.

Taking young boys and expecting them to work like twenty-year-olds is a challenge for them and for me. I push them hard, and at times past their abilities both physically and mentally. However, these guys have accepted the work and show up again the next day ready for more. They have entered a man's world. I'm pleased with them.

One particularly important lesson is hard for every boy to learn. It marks the difference between a poor worker and an excellent one. Davey, because he's the youngest, has had the toughest time grasping it.

"Davey, I want you to sweep out the front bedroom," I command.

Half an hour later he comes back and says, "I'm all done."

I walk into the room to inspect it. "Hey, what about that block of wood, look at the sawdust in the corners and along the edge? What do you mean, you're done?"

Davey begins his excuses, "I didn't see that block. I can't get the broom in the corners. It's too hard."

I give him a few tips on sweeping and leave him to his work while I return to mine.

"Hey Boss."

"What, Davey?"

"I'm done with the room."

I enter to inspect again. "Davey, why did you leave that corner undone?"

"Oh, I missed that one."

"Then you are not finished. Try again and call me when you are finished."

On another day, I sent Nathan around the outside of the house to see if there were any nails missing in the plywood sheathing. After two hours of nailing he announced that he was done. Then, I sent Paul around to do the same thing. After an hour, he came back to say he was finished.

When the county inspector showed up to inspect the plywood nailing, I met him at his car. "I want to teach these boys a lesson," I said. "They've missed many places that should be nailed. Please be tough on them, show them clearly what they missed and why that shouldn't happen."

When the inspector drove away, Nathan sheepishly said, "That was embarrassing." The boys had failed to finish their job, as the inspector clearly pointed out.

I sent the inspector after the boys because I want them to learn to finish their tasks. Why? Because if they don't *completely* nail a brace, another worker could lean on it and fall from the roof. If they don't remove *all* the nails sticking up from a board, someone could step on it. If they don't nail *all* the joints on the roof sheathing, in two years it will buckle up and leave an unsightly hump in the roof.

For the sake of the building and for safety, a worker cannot fail to finish the tasks given to him.

The best reason for thoroughly completing our work is that God thoroughly completes His work. If we want to learn to walk with Him, we need to accept our assignments with a mind to finish them because that's the way He lives.

Jesus is the example of what our attitude and actions should be. When asked if He had anything to eat, Jesus answered, "My meat is to do the will of him that sent me, and to finish his work" (John 4:34). He didn't come to earth just to put in His time. He had a job to do and set out to complete it. When responding to the attacks of the Jewish leaders, Jesus said, "the works which the Father hath given me to finish, the same works...I do" (John 5:36). God didn't send Jesus to work at something. He gave Him a job He wanted done. The very last words Jesus spoke before He died were, "It is finished" (John 19:30).

Aren't you glad that Jesus didn't work halfheartedly at saving you from sin? We have confidence that He is able to save us to the uttermost because He finishes what He starts.

We are created in God's image. Therefore He intends for us to have a mind to finish our work, just as He does. You don't have to be on a building site to learn to finish your tasks. When your parents ask you to clean your room, it's an opportunity to align with God by completing the work. You don't want to be sidetracked by a magazine or by playing with something you'd lost months before under the trash. When you have a task to do, put your whole heart into it until it's done.

This week when I asked Davey to pick up the electrician's scraps, he systematically set out to finish the job and thoroughly completed it. He's growing up, becoming an asset to the crew, and we all enjoy seeing him develop a mind to work.

If you follow this simple tip of finishing each task assigned to you, every employer in town will want you to work for him. Your parents will be thrilled. What is more, you will hear your Father in heaven say, "Well done, thou good and faithful servant: thou hast been faithful over a few things, I will make thee ruler over many things: enter thou into the joy of thy lord" (Matthew 25:21).

Wherefore he is able also to save them to the uttermost that come unto God by him, seeing he ever liveth to make intercession for them. (Hebrews 7:25)

Questions

- What happened when I asked Davey to sweep the front bedroom?

- What quality does every employer look for in a worker?

- Why should we finish the tasks given to us?

- What task did Jesus finish?

- What reward does God offer to those who finish their tasks?

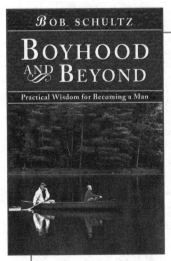

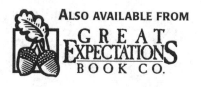
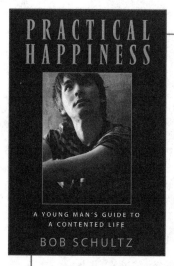

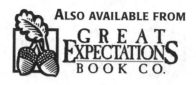

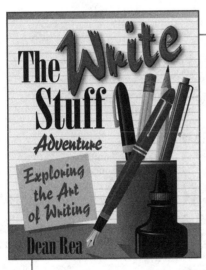

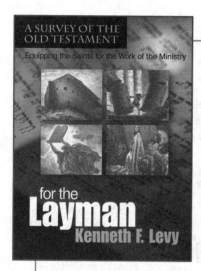

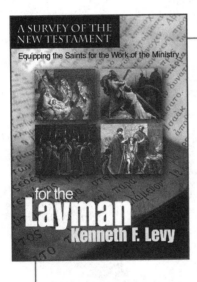

ORDER FORM

Quantity	Title	Each	Total
	Created for Work — ISBN 1-883934-11-7	$10.99	
	Boyhood and Beyond — ISBN 1-883934-09-5	$10.99	
	Practical Happiness — ISBN 978-1-883934-13-2	$10.99	
	Beautiful Girlhood — ISBN 1-883934-02-8	$8.99	
	Hints on Child Training — ISBN 1-883934-01-X	$8.99	
	The Write Stuff Adventure — ISBN 1-883934-04-4	$19.99	
	For the Layman: A Survey of the Old Testament ISBN 1-883934-05-2	$24.99	
	For the Layman: A Survey of the Old Testament additional workbook — ISBN 1-883934-07-9	$11.99	
	For the Layman: A Survey of the New Testament ISBN 1-883934-06-0	$24.99	
	For the Layman: A Survey of the New Testament additional workbook — ISBN 1-883934-08-7	$11.99	

Ship To:
Name: _____

Address: _____

_____

Merchandise Total	
Shipping & Handling	
Total Enclosed	

Please make checks payable to:
Great Expectations Book Company
P.O. Box 2067
Eugene, Oregon 97402

You may also order online at:
www.gebconline.com

Shipping & Handling Information:

$2.50 for the first book, 1.00 for each additional book to the same address.

$2.50 for each book sent to a separate address.

CANADA: $4.00 for the first book, $1.75 for each additional book to the same address.
U.S. currency only.
$4.00 for each book sent to a separate address
U.S. currency only.